To:

_____

From:

_____

2020
VISION
DEVOTIONAL

I Can See Clearly Now
A 40-Day Devotional

Shauna-kaye Brown

2020 VISION DEVOTIONAL

ISBN: 978-0-578-65595-6

Published by SHAUNA-KAYE BROWN

(Manifest Your Greatness Now)

First Edition: February 2020

For Worldwide Distribution, Printed in the U.S.A.

For information on booking the author for speaking engagements, interviews, book signings, and other events, please contact Shauna-kaye Brown @ www.shaunakbrownspeaks.com

DEDICATION

This book is dedicated to all the individuals who need a **word** to get them through the day. Know that God is not through with you yet. If you have this devotional in your hands, you are well placed to receive one of the greatest gifts one could ever ask for, the opportunity for a **fresh start**. I hope you realize you have everything you need to begin to manifest your greatness **Now**!

ACKNOWLEDGMENT

I give all glory to the Holy Spirit for His guidance and strength throughout this journey. Without His grace, this devotional would not have been possible.

Thank you to my Pastor and spiritual leaders who inspired the forty-day fast that sparked this book. Your wisdom challenged me to grow deeper in faith. Also, to my family and friends, your prayers and support carried me through moments of doubt. Your encouragement means the world to me. I am grateful to my mentors, coaches, and colleagues who helped sharpen my vision and pushed me toward greater purpose.

To you, the reader, thank you for embracing this message. May it inspire you to pursue your extraordinary vision with boldness and faith.

Finally, thanks to all who contributed in one way or another behind the scenes, encouragers, prayer partners, and supporters. Your efforts have made this devotional a reality.

With gratitude,
Shauna-kaye Brown

CONTENTS

INTRODUCTION

In the year 2020, a powerful truth became even clearer to me: one who has a vision is far more likely to reach their intended destination than one who wanders aimlessly. It is that straightforward. Proverbs 29:18 reminds us, *"Where there is no vision, the people perish."* Yet, despite this timeless wisdom, countless individuals continue to live lives that barely scratch the surface of existence, lacking purpose, direction, or a clear sense of destiny.

Earl Nightingale once said, *"A man without a goal is like a ship without a rudder."* Imagine that ship, drifting on an endless sea, at the mercy of the winds and waves, vulnerable to ending up not where it was meant to be but lost somewhere among the forgotten. Without a clear vision or goal, life becomes little more than survival, a state of constant striving, rather than thriving.

However, while pursuing a grand vision is essential, it is equally important to avoid the trap of relentless striving that blinds us to the present moment. If we become consumed with chasing more, we risk losing the very life unfolding right now. Progress is not just about reaching goals; it is also about embracing each step with awareness and gratitude.

In December of 2019, when our Pastor announced a 40-day fast beginning January 2020, I was ready to embrace the challenge. Yet I was honest with myself. I had never fasted for more than one week, and even that had been a struggle. How would I endure forty days? The only option was to pray earnestly for divine strength. I knew from my unique relationship with food that I needed more than willpower; I needed God's intervention. So, I committed myself to seeking the Lord's guidance on how to navigate this spiritual journey successfully.

Much like my prayer life, my fasting life required a transformation. If someone had asked me, *"Shauna-kaye, is your fasting life hot or cold?"* I would have answered that it was neither hot nor cold, perhaps just lukewarm. That realization propelled me to intentionally pursue a deeper, more committed spiritual discipline if I was to grow in faith and purpose.

One of my key goals for the year 2020 was to cultivate a more intimate, profound relationship with God. I understood that my spiritual vision demanded radical renewal. Ordinary "2020 vision" was no longer enough. For those who understand optometry, 20/20 vision represents normal clarity, but extraordinary vision is 20/10. I recall a Sunday service with **Bishop George Bloomer**, where he shared that the year 2010 symbolized the era for extraordinary visions and miracles, consistent with the science of sight. In comparison, 2020 represented a time of ordinary visions and miracles. Yet here we are, well beyond 2010, and many are still searching for those extraordinary revelations.

I am a firm believer in the power of the present moment. The only time we truly have is now. How we choose to engage with this moment shapes the magnitude of miracles we experience. This book, 2020 Vision Devotional, was born out of the conviction that every single day is a miracle. The sooner we embrace this reality, the more we will live lives fueled by purpose and clarity.

For me, 2020 is no longer just a year in the past. A moment ago, is not just that moment, it was once now, and suddenly it is no more. Each moment we have represents a symbol of extraordinary vision, the here and now, because what we do in this moment is entirely within our power. After forty days of fasting and prayer, I gained clarity far beyond ordinary sight, and it compelled me to share these revelations with you, one word at a time. Hence the book you now have in your possession. The Word reminds us, *"If thou canst believe, all things are possible to him that believeth."* (Mark 9:23). This statement highlights the centrality of faith in the life of a believer. Jesus is addressing the father of a boy possessed by an unclean spirit, emphasizing that belief is the key that unlocks divine power and possibility. The phrase *"all things are possible"* does not imply a naive or wishful thinking, but rather a profound trust in God's limitless ability to act in and through our lives. True belief is not merely intellectual assent but a heartfelt confidence that God can overcome any obstacle. This verse calls believers to surrender doubt and embrace faith as the foundation for experiencing God's miraculous intervention.

Let us pray

Father, thank You for the vision to see clearly what I must do to gain true clarity. Open the eyes of my understanding so that I may appreciate each waking moment as a precious miracle. Teach me to focus deeply on my spiritual growth as I allow my life to be transformed through the renewing of my mind. I thank You for Your guidance and grace. In Jesus' name, I pray. Amen.

DAY 1

VISION

Vision literally refers to having the faculty or ability to see. However, here we are not so much concerned with physical vision, but your aptitude for thinking about or planning your future with unreserved imagination and wisdom. To dispel any uncertainties about this position, understand that even with your unique vision, you must be fully prepared to submit to the will of God.

Understand also, that the vision you have is for an appointed time. Therefore, do not be discouraged because you don't see results within the time you have set for yourself. Never lose sight of the fact that God's timing is perfect. It is not your will but God's will that must prevail.

Habakkuk 2:3 tells us, *"For the vision is yet for an appointed time, but at the end it shall speak, and not lie; though it tarry, wait for it; because it will surely come."* Here, the prophets and other men had harboured doubts about the fulfillment of prophecies owing to the extended period of time they had to wait. Likewise, many times we envision a result occurring within a particular time and are disappointed when it is not achieved. This verse is a timely reminder that every vision has an appointed time. However, the appointed time is not always what you deemed to be the right time. In this case, the prophets and other great men were being reminded that this appointed time was not just for the present vision, but visions and prophecies in general.

I take personal responsibility in entreating you to continue to believe. Do not allow doubt to seep in even when everything may look bleak. Wait for your big vision to come to fruition at the opportune time as God's word will not return to Him void but will accomplish that to which it was sent. Though you may be made to wait longer than anticipated, remember;

> *God is not a man, that he should lie; neither the son of man, that he should repent: hath he said, and shall he not do it? or hath he spoken, and shall he not make it good?* (Numbers 23:19)

This scripture refers to God's promise to his people Israel that they would inherit a land of their own (Canaan). They were assured happiness and a promised land to call home. Yet we see where they had to tarry for forty years before this was realized. One thing I want you to understand is, there are times we are made to wait because of our own disobedience. In setting your big vision, it helps to stay focused and attuned to God's will in the larger purpose so you will not deviate from it. Ask the Holy Spirit, what is your will concerning this?

One more thing, do not be afraid to set a scary vision. This speaks to your trust and faith in God. Don't limit your vision to the ability you perceive by your present circumstances. Allow me to share five considerations when setting your big vision:

1. **Pray about it:** Prayer helps to clarify your ideas and assess whether they are worth pursuing.
2. **Write it down:** When you write down what you envisage, it becomes real to you. Now you have something to work toward.
3. **Take action:** It is not enough that you have written it down, now you must be prepared for the arduous

task of getting it done.

4. **Do not be discouraged:** It is common to get discouraged and harbour doubt throughout your journey. This is heightened by the fact that human beings have a propensity to get impatient.

5. **Express gratitude:** *"In every thing give thanks: for this is the will of God in Christ Jesus concerning you,"* (1 Thessalonians 5:18, NKJV). We are asked to give thanks in everything we do. The operative word here is 'in'.

Even in the midst of your adversities and disappointments, give thanks, because often these are strategically placed to help you along your journey to the 'Big Vision'. The enemy who is prowling, looking for souls to devour lays in wait for you to make a mistake so he can attack you. You must be mindful of this as you grow through your trials. The plan of the enemy should never deter you from tapping into the greatness implanted in you. It is your vision, and crazy as it may sound, you were brought here to realize it. If you fail to press on, you do yourself and those you were called to serve a disservice.

Create a vision for the life you really want and then work relentlessly towards making it a reality. (Roy T. Bennett)

The above quote cuts straight to the heart of purposeful living. It challenges you to get crystal clear about what you truly desire, not what others expect or what is convenient, but your authentic vision for your life. Vision is the blueprint; it gives direction and meaning. But having a vision alone is not enough. The second part demands relentless action, consistent, determined effort without excuses or distractions. Dreams do not materialize on their own; they require discipline, focus, and resilience. This quote is a call to stop waiting, stop hesitating, and start grinding toward your goals with unwavering commitment. Your vision is only as powerful as the work you put into it.

Reflection

What is your vision for this year/this moment?

_____

_____

_____

_____

Now that you have decided what you want to accomplish, what can you do differently to achieve that result?

_____

_____

_____

_____

_____

_____

DAY 2

SIGHT

In the words of **Bishop Justice Kojo Bentil,** *"we see with our spirit, but we look with our eyes. If we are to see who we are in the Lord; we would not dwell on the present but on what the Bible says about us."* Here, I am not suggesting that you should extricate yourself from the present. Remaining spiritually present is when you are most likely to be in touch with who you are in Christ. My objective is to encourage you to look beyond your present reality, especially if it appears unfavourable and see yourself as God sees you, see yourself as a child of God created in his image and likeness. (Genesis 1:27).

The word of God is replete with commendations about human beings and their potential. Yet, we often spend an excessive amount of time dwelling on the things that tend to limit us such as; not enough money, not being born in the right family or not having enough people who believe in us.

As **Dr. Wayne Dyer** proffers, human beings have a proclivity to always want *more* so we are seldom satisfied with what we have right now. I am impelled to remind you that even in the presence of grave distress, your God-given potential is still inside you.

In John 15:5 (NKJV) God says, *"I am the vine, you are the branches. He who abides in Me, and I in him, bears much fruit; for without Me you can do nothing."* I use this analogy of the tree and its branches to show that as children of the Father, we are not separate from God. If we stay in the word of God and apply it to our lives, our paths to abundance become certain. However, if we see ourselves as separate from God, it becomes hard for us to perceive a reality where God dwells in us and we are under his constant protection.

> *Having the eyes of your hearts enlightened, that you may know what is the hope to which he has called you, what are the riches of his glorious inheritance in the saints,* (Ephesians 1:18, ESV).

Though this verse is concerned with an inheritance of eternal life, we are made to realize that spiritual sight or enlightenment is ultimately responsible for our appreciation of God's promises to us. Sight then refers not only to our physical ability to see but our spiritual purview concerning the will of God for our lives.

When we see ourselves only as others see us, we are seldom able to see beyond our needs and circumstances. What if I tell you that these are the same limiting beliefs which operate to keep us where we are right now. When you begin to see yourself as God sees you, then you also realize that physical sight is only one dimension through which to see yourself as well as the rest of the world.

Suppose you were to change your perspective and begin to look at yourself through God's eyes. You would realize that God sees you as precious and unique and of great value.

The question is, how do you see yourself? Is your purview of yourself inhibiting you from reaching your highest potential? One of our greatest hindrances is, we often see ourselves only through the lenses of our physical eyes instead of as God sees us.

Let us pray

Father, thank you for the gift of spiritual sight. I place my supplication before You. Open the eyes of my understanding so I will see myself and my abilities as You do. I know that you have called me to realize a big vision for the edification of others and ultimately for Your glory. Thank you for this assignment. Thank you, Lord. In Jesus' name, I pray. Amen.

DAY 3

PROBATION

Most of you are familiar with the creation story as depicted in the book of Genesis. Here we learn that owing to the fall of man from God's grace, we inherited a world in which sin had entered. (Genesis 3:6). But how many of you actually put this early period of man's fall from grace into perspective?

A few weeks ago, I had the distinct pleasure of meeting with and learning from a man full of knowledge and godly wisdom who helped me to gain some insights into this matter. It is this newly acquired understanding that I want to share with you today. As you know, probation refers to a process or period of testing or observing the character or abilities of a person in a specific role. Commonly seen is the new employee who needs to be assessed over a period of time, to decipher whether he or she is suitable for the specific job responsibilities. Now, what if I tell you that Adam and his help-meet Eve, were on probation during the initial period of mankind on earth? Yes, they were being tested by God to see whether they were ready for the mammoth responsibility God had bestowed on them. Remember, He made man and gave him dominion over all the things of the earth.

In your pursuit of purpose, God puts you through a period of testing in order to fortify you and ensure you are ready to be used by Him. If you fail your probation, your purpose could easily be thwarted or diverted. Remember, you overcome by the blood of the lamb and by the power of your testimony. (Revelation 12:11). Your tests are what give rise to your testimony. In Genesis 2:15, we see where, *"...the LORD God took the man, and put him into the garden of Eden to dress it and to keep it."* Man was placed in the Garden of Eden to watch over it, tend to it and make it his permanent and settled dwelling. One of the most important lessons which is evident from this verse is that from the inception, man was afforded a God-given purpose.

However, Adam and Eve had to prove themselves through this period of testing and they failed.

12

From the creation story in Genesis 3, we see where Eve succumbed to the serpent's deception and disobeyed God's command. During a period of testing, if you do not perform as expected by your employer or your supervisor, you may not be recommended for a permanent position, or, even if you are recommended the terms may change. In their case, though Adam and Eve did not immediately face death, the terms of their dominion over everything on the earth changed. They were banished from the Garden of Eden. (Genesis 3:24).

God our Father and His Son Jesus Christ, with their perfect foreknowledge, already recommended every one of you to fill your mortal probation during the most decisive period in the history of the world. (Sheri L. Dew)

Arguably, your entire earthly life is a period of probation which means you will be tested often. Therefore, as you embark on your purposeful life journey, understand that life is a process you are meant to experience and learn from. If things are not working out as you have anticipated, it may be because your probationary period is not yet over. Remember, on the first day when you started this process you were entreated to have a large vision. As is the usual case with large visions, challenges are inevitable. Remember;

You are the descendants of the prophets and of the covenant that God gave to your ancestors, saying to Abraham, 'And in your descendants, all the families of the earth shall be blessed.
(Acts 3:25, NRSV)

If you are blessed, then any tests that you are going through, no matter how difficult, is temporary. Your period of probation is not there to discourage you from your vision, but to fortify you as you work toward its realization. Realization comes from us denying ourselves daily in order to commit to Christ through our obedience. We may think this is one of the longest periods of probation one could face, but in the end, it will be worth it. Probation is simply one of life's inevitabilities created to fortify you.

Reflection

How can you work through your period of probation and ensure your purpose is fulfilled?

_____

_____

_____

_____

_____

DAY 4

ADVERSITY

Proverbs 24:10 admonishes, *"If you faint in the day of adversity, your strength is small."* I know for some; this statement is like a harsh reproach because many adverse situations we face are so tough that one feels like they cannot help but succumb. Yet, the scripture is clear, if you don't withstand the adversity, you are essentially weak. Knowing that God has given us the power to remain standing even in the worse of storms can help us to endure the pressure.

> *We are afflicted in every way, but not crushed; perplexed, but not driven to despair; persecuted, but not forsaken; struck down, but not destroyed;* (2 Corinthians 4:8-9, ESV)

Here, the Apostle Paul vividly describes the paradox of the Christian experience amid suffering. "*We are afflicted in every way,*

15

but not crushed" acknowledges the full spectrum of hardships believers face, yet emphasizes that these trials do not ultimately defeat them. The *phrase "perplexed, but not driven to despair"* reveals that while believers may be confused or challenged by circumstances, they do not lose hope or abandon faith. *"Persecuted, but not forsaken"* points to external opposition and hostility, yet God's presence remains steadfast, ensuring they are never abandoned. Finally, *"struck down, but not destroyed"* highlights that despite setbacks or physical suffering, the inner spirit remains resilient and alive. This passage captures the sustaining power of God's grace, which preserves believers through adversity and secures their ultimate victory despite temporary hardships.

So, the question is, how do you acquire the kind of determination and perseverance that makes you thrive in the face of adversity? I recommend fasting and prayer. In the book of Matthew 6, Jesus said to his disciples, *"… when you fast, do not be like the hypocrites, with a sad countenance."* Implicit in this scripture is the idea that the disciples will be fasting. This is indicated by the word 'when'.

Even though Jesus was not telling them that they must fast, he cautioned then on how they should do it when they did fast. Fasting teaches discipline and self-control because, during those moments, you abstain from food or things which often capture your attention sometimes even to your detriment. With fasting, you develop the strength and self-restraint to forego even that which you love. This is simply a process of fortification necessary for you to move to the next level.

Matthew 6 also addresses how we should pray. Jesus' disciples observed His practices and noticed that he spent a lot of time praying. Though they could have asked Him how to perform miracles, they must have realized that there was some power in praying given the amount of time Jesus spent in the secret place of prayer. I submit that if you want to thrive in times of hardship, you must spend time fortifying yourself.

> *One who gains strength by overcoming obstacles possesses the only strength which can overcome adversity.* Albert Schweitzer)

When troubles and trials come, we need to be like Stephen and stand up for what is right, not what seems easy. Truthfully, it is easy to talk about strength and grit when all is going well. Perhaps, if we were tested as Peter was during

Jesus' crucifixion, we might become so afraid that we would run and hide. Still, you must stand!

Reflection

What are your tools of fortification? How do you measure their effectiveness in times of adversity?

_____

_____

_____

_____

_____

DAY 5

TRADITION

Most people who have followed my work for an extended period know that I am not inclined to set New Year's Resolutions. Yet, for many people, setting resolutions is a time-honoured tradition. Truthfully, most times when you make a vow to dramatically transform your life at the beginning of the year, you seldom ever commit to these grandiose plans. I find that making a commitment to change, should not be confined to a specific time of year. Change is inevitable, but it is the compound effect of any action that will signify a real sense of change in your life.

Therefore, do not throw away your confidence, which has a great reward. For you have need of endurance, so that when

you have done the will of God you may receive what is
promised. (Hebrews 10:35-36, ESV)

Your entire life is a test of endurance and one key requirement is that we have a surfeit of patience. Yet, more often than not we tend to abandon our course because we set unrealistic timelines and then hastily look for results. When you focus on doing the will of God, even in setting goals for transformation, you have more clarity thus shifting your focus from a specific time of year to obeying God's will.

> *It is a fine thing to establish one's own religion in one's heart,*
> *not to be dependent on tradition and second-hand ideals. Life*
> *will seem to you, later, not a lesser, but a greater thing.* (D.H.
> Lawrence)

Focus on developing your own tradition of setting goals and understand that you have an opportunity to grow every single day of your life.

What do you think about setting New Year's Resolutions? Do you find that they work for you?

Here's what I think, if one wishes to embark on a new journey or a new way of doing things, they should do so whenever the urge arises. Making this a beginning of the year agenda can do more harm than good. Thus, in lieu of setting New Year's Resolutions, I set goals. When you set goals and institute a plan of action, you are more likely to see results than when you choose the confinement of the proverbial resolutions. Not only that, you can focus on living daily instead of constantly striving.

Without counsel, plans fail, but with many advisers, they succeed. (Proverbs 15:22, ESV)

Focus your attention on seeking mentorship from your mentors and spiritual teachers. As you seek to establish your plans in God, He will send you destiny helpers along the way.

In their hearts, humans plan their course, but the LORD establishes their steps. (Proverbs 16:9, NIV)

As you know setting resolutions is a tradition most common in the Western Hemisphere though also found in the Eastern Hemisphere. Irrespective of where it is practiced, the key behind this custom is individuals resolve to alter certain unfavorable traits, accomplish key goals or simply implement strategies to change their lives. However, the sinking feeling one gets when after just a few short weeks or months, they veer off track, is hard to recover from. Worry can cause us to lose even more time as we become disheartened in the process and sometimes may even give up on ourselves prematurely.

Who of you by worrying can add a single hour to your life? (Luke 12:25, NIV)

Reflection

What are some of the transformational goals you have set for yourself? Outline some steps you will take toward the daily accomplishment of those goals.

_____

_____

_____

_____

_____

_____

DAY 6

PREPARATION

We should live our lives as though Christ was coming this afternoon. (Jimmy Carter)

One way to perceive your journey here on earth is as a prolonged period of preparation for eternity. **Rick Warren** in <u>A Purpose Driven Life</u> tells us that in order to live our lives with purpose we must see fellowship and worship as parts of our responsibility to secure eternal life. In that case, we are expected to incorporate these two requirements in our daily pursuits after righteousness.

Simply put, we must prepare ourselves for the day of judgment just as Jesus has gone to prepare a place for us that when He returns, He can receive us to himself. His goal is to ensure that we will be with Him always. (John 14:3)

Before you apply for a job, you usually prepare a resume and cover letter to submit to your potential employer. If they are pleased with what you present on paper, they might call you in for a face-to-face interview. Again, you spend quality time preparing for that interview. You try to preempt any questions you think they might ask you and you chose an attire fit for an interview. In this instance, you recognize that you are more likely to find favor with the interviewers if you are ready.

> *Opportunity does not waste time with those who are unprepared.* (Idowu Koyenikan)

There are many dimensions to getting oneself ready for any responsibility. Therefore, sometimes you are intentional about your process and at other times, even the adverse experiences serve as part of your preparation.

> *And it came to pass when Joseph was come unto his brethren, that they stript Joseph out of his coat, his coat of many colours that was on him; And they took him, and cast him into a pit: and the pit was empty, there was no water in it.* (Genesis 37:23-24)

Here, Joseph's brothers strip him of his *"coat of many colours,"* a symbol of their father's special favor and Joseph's unique identity. This act of removing the coat signifies rejection and betrayal by those closest to him. Casting Joseph into an empty pit represents a place of abandonment and despair, highlighting the depth of their hostility. The absence of water in the pit underscores the harshness of his situation, he is trapped in a lifeless, isolating place. These verses foreshadow the trials Joseph will endure, yet they also set the stage for God's providential plan to unfold through adversity.

In looking at Joseph's experience in Egypt, we see that even before he got there, he faced adversities that could have taken his life. For me, the worse part of Joseph's challenges did not come from strangers, but from his own family. Likewise, many times we suffer hardships at the hands of our own family and friends. Even then, I urge you to remember Joseph who despite his adversities; being left for dead in a pit by his brothers and being sold as a slave in Egypt, he became a ruler in the land of his oppressors. (Genesis 37)

Not only that but at their most destitute moments, Joseph gave a home to his people. Do not be surprised if God uses you to rescue the same people who fought you *en route* to your destiny. The important thing to remember as you are being challenged is, when God calls you for greatness, you must endure a period of preparation. It is in such moments that you grow and become ready for your assignment. Stay strong!

Reflection

Do you think you will learn to treat your adversities differently after reading this excerpt about preparation?

_____

_____

_____

_____

_____

_____

DAY 7

DOUBTS

Rollo May, a distinguished psychologist, once said,

the relationship between commitment and doubt is by no means an antagonistic one. Commitment is healthiest when it's not without doubt but in spite of doubt.

As you go after life's ideals, doubt is one of the inevitabilities you will face. However, just because you have a doubt, it doesn't mean you should not commit. Of course, I know that when doubt arises, the hardest part of the journey is to continue in the face of it, yet you must. Many people fail because they stop at the point of uncertainty.

Our doubts are traitors and make us lose the good we oft might win, by fearing to attempt. (William Shakespeare)

We often associate fear with one's failure to venture into the unknown or attempt something outside of the proverbial comfort zone. Yet, doubt I believe is an equal imposter. Because of doubt, many great men and women have gone on to live mediocre lives, not because of the absence of ability, but the presence of uncertainty.

Sir William Shakespeare captures the reason behind such inaction quite appropriately. It has been impressed upon me to nudge you into action even where you have a strong sense of distrust for the unknown. If you are to grow beyond your comfort zone, you must be willing to stretch beyond your known limit.

In Jesus' introduction into Ministry, we saw where He uses the *'miraculous draught of fishes'* to show rather than tell the people who He was. It was at this time that He also chose His first disciples. In Luke 5, we saw where Simon, an experienced fisherman who after being taught by Jesus was told to cast his net into the sea. *"...he said unto Simon, launch out into the deep, and let down your nets."* (Luke 5:5). In Simon's response to this instruction, he appeared somewhat irritated when Jesus told him to cast his net. This may have been because of his experience as a fisherman, or the fact that he had toiled all night to no avail. Also, fishing is most effective at night time. Certainly, his doubt could have been due to his wealth of experience as a fisherman. Likewise, we often doubt moving in certain directions because of what we know or what we think we know. Today I commission you to 'let down your nets' even in face of doubt. Again, this feeling of doubt which threatens to prod you into inaction is not unique to you. It is the reason behind so many people remaining unexceptional while the three percent account for the truly successful.

Another thing, do not feel like because you are a Christian and you harbor doubt, that makes you less than your brothers and sisters. The next time such a thought crosses your mind, remember, you are not alone. After all, doubt is nothing new and is not partial to the unrighteous. In the book of Luke, we see where Zechariah expressed doubt when the angel Gabriel appeared to him in the temple.

> *Zechariah asked the angel, "How can I be sure of this? I am an old man and my wife is well along in years.* (Luke 1:18, NIV)

This story proves that even Zechariah the priest was not exempt from being uncertain. He was clearly doubtful when the angel told him about the coming of his son John. This shows that as human beings, we are fallible.

Therefore, despite our proportions of faith and righteousness, doubt can still creep in. What is important is remaining committed in the face of uncertainty. Commitment is an action word, therefore, instead of cautious inaction, take care to do just a little each day. Doubt will not inhibit you from your pursuit of purpose, in Jesus's name.

Ultimately, I have found, the difference between those who succeed and those who fail is not natural talents or being born to the right family, but persevering in the midst of uncertainty, doubt, and fear. You are no different, you can do that!

Reflection

How has doubt prevented you from acting on your ideas? After reading today's word, how will you push yourself beyond your comfort zone to work on your goals?

_____

_____

_____

_____

DAY 8

SEEK

Rick Warren, the author of <u>A Purpose Driven Life</u> once said, *"the most common mistake Christians make in worship today is seeking an experience rather than seeking God."* I often have discussions with my learned friends about different aspects of the word of God and what they mean to teach us.

As disciples, we understand that the word of God captured in the sixty-six books of the Bible is the manual for human understanding and living. Much like when you buy an appliance or an electronic device, they come with a manual that guides you as to how to assemble and operate them. Likewise, the Bible tells us how God expects us to live as disciples on earth.

Recently, I had a discussion with a dear friend about some of the things we struggle with as Christians. At the moment when I was giving him my 'two cents,' it occurred to me that I didn't really have the answer to his queries, not directly. In that instant, I commissioned him and I suppose myself, to seek the insight of the holy spirit on the matter. Matthew 6:33 urges us to seek God first above everything else,

> *But seek first his kingdom and his righteousness, and all these things will be given to you as well.* (Matthew 6:33, NIV)

I think when we get to know God and we start to walk in righteousness, this will be our ammunition to deal with the things that Galatians 5 tells us to stay away from on the one hand, and how we should govern our lives on the other. *"But I say, walk by the Spirit, and you will not carry out the desire of the flesh."* (Galatians 5:16, NASB).

When we walk in the Spirit, we receive the fortitude to stand up against temptations and urges. Yet, one does not walk in the spirit as of right. Instead, it is through steadfastly seeking God that one reaches this zenith.

In our daily lives, we grapple with things that threaten to take us off our divine course. Today, I urge you to consider seeking God's face for direction as you press on to your higher calling!

I am seeking, I am striving, I am in it with all my heart. (Van Gogh)

Let us pray

Lord, teach me how to seek you. My greatest desire is to serve you with all my heart and to walk in complete obedience. I pray that as I learn to seek you first, I will begin to walk in holiness always. Father, you are my rock and my fortress and I desire to submit to your will. In Jesus' name, men.

DAY 9

EXPECTATION

Now faith is the substance of things hoped for, the evidence of things not seen. (Hebrews 11:1)

When you leverage your faith regarding the vision you have for your life, you assume the position of power. Your experiences no longer lurk in the shadows threatening to pounce on you at your unawares. Your faith heightens your belief that the things you have envisioned will be manifested on the physical plane. Even if they do not, you extrapolate the lessons learned and you move forward with greater power, the power of knowing more than you did before.

According to **Brian Tracy,** *"positive expectations are the mark of the superior personality."* It doesn't mean because your expectations are positive, your results will be ideal. However, having such expectations allow you to view the world from a different perspective. With this purview, you develop the tendency to go about your life without hindrance or fear.

You are not made into a superior being, but a confident one expecting favorable results. The Bible encourages those who trust in the Lord to expect good things from Him. *"My soul, wait thou only upon God; for my expectation is from him"* (Psalm 62:5).

Many people fail to achieve greatness because they are operating out of their experiences instead of their expectations. Experiences can sometimes be so devastating that one becomes immobilized with fear of messing up or failing again. Getting a person who has become crippled with fear to get back on track is very difficult. This is why changing your outcomes also requires a change in perspective. This begins with learning to live and thrive with the things you cannot change. And, try as you may, you cannot alter your past experiences but you can visualize the outcome you desire. This, in essence, is what amounts to expectations.

Oprah Winfrey commissions us to turn our wounds into wisdom. Likewise, we have often heard it said, 'experience teaches wisdom'. But does it always? I believe for you to garner wisdom from your experiences, it takes some amount of deliberate effort. Implicit in Oprah's statement is the idea that you have the ability (power) to turn your wounds into wisdom, but it is a choice which you must make.

> *Hope is favorable and confident expectation; it's an expectant attitude that something good is going to happen and things will work out, no matter what situation we're facing.* (Joyce Meyer)

Do you remember a book by **Charles Dickens** called Great Expectations? In the book, the protagonist, *'Pip'* expected money to buy him happiness as well as a social position as a gentleman, and love. He was not prepared for the moral lessons which he was eventually forced to accept. He soon realized that the most valuable things in life are priceless, money cannot buy love, happiness nor human ethical values. Even so, operating in a spirit of expectation allowed him to rise above the ordinary and become a gentleman in society.

Reflection

Do you find that when you are expectant, your outcomes tend to be more favorable? How can you leverage a mindset of expectation to acquire the things you seek after in your life?

_____

_____

_____

_____

_____

_____

_____

DAY 10

PERSPECTIVE

"To change ourselves effectively, we first had to change our perceptions."
Stephen R. Covey. Today, my demeanor is naturally inclined to search for the bright side and pay little regard to things that make everyone else unhappy.

In case you are wondering or you had met me twenty years ago and is utterly confused about my statement, I was not always this way. I spent a long time being mindful of what others think about me and being offended by people who treated me poorly. That is how I moved from day-to-day until one day I had an epiphany. I must have been about thirteen years old and had by then grown tired of all the sadness around me. Even then, I realized, there are so many variables in operation that are out of my control. So many, that if I was not careful, I would continue to exist in perpetual melancholy with only a few glimpses of happiness.

> *For our light and momentary troubles are achieving for us an eternal glory that far outweighs them all. So, we fix our eyes not on what is seen, but on what is unseen, since what is seen is temporary, but what is unseen is eternal.* (2 Corinthians 4:17-18, NIV)

How could I hold on to my moments of contentment if the world around me was in a constant state of upheaval? It was during a mission to answer this question that I had what felt like a divine revelation. I remember I was supposed to have an end of term test in Religious Education. I was not fully prepared and the day of the test was literally right around the corner. I recall thinking, if only I had a little more time and then suddenly, the rain came. It was heavy, and back then when it rained heavily, our school would be dismissed early or we would get a day off. As **Les Brown** said, *"the universe unfolds as it should,"* my test was postponed and at last, I had enough time to prepare. I was so relieved!

Dr. Wayne Dyer once said, *"when we change the way we look at things, the things we look at change."* As I sat on my great grandfather's grave studying for my test, I thought about how things unfolded and realized, there are so many things in life one cannot control that we should take the reins on the ones we can.

At that moment, I made a decision that moving forward I would take control of my happiness. To do this, I decided to look for the good in all people and situations.

This changed my whole perspective and now, often I find myself on the other side of what makes others miserable and unhappy. For that, I have been called self-righteous, fake, unrealistic and even eccentric. I cannot argue with the latter, but I would not change my way for anything. If you really believed that, *"every cloud has a silver lining,"* then you would see why I am this way today. If not, stop saying things you don't mean! What silver lining?

Clarity of vision is an invaluable asset which if one possesses it can alter their lives forever. In the same breath, a cynical and sarcastic perspective on everything will not get you where you want to go. You must learn to gain the right perspective on issues, the one that will put you in a position to win. Change your perspective, change your life.

Reflection

How do you view the people and events in the world around you? Do you find that if you change your perspective, things that were once hopeless begin to appear promising?

_____

_____

_____

_____

_____

_____

DAY 11

JOY

For believers who have had a personal encounter with the Holy Spirit, when thinking about their heavenly inheritance, they do so joyously. In 1 Peter 8-9, we are told that, though now we do not see *God,* yet believing, we rejoice with joy inexpressible and full of glory. This is for those who can vividly envision what will transpire for the righteous when Jesus returns.

> *Your JOY comes from how you think, the choices that we make in life.* (Joyce Meyer)

But what is joy? Very often we see that in expressing what the essence of joy is, writers often juxtapose it with happiness. One's attention is then drawn to the disparity between the two to establish why one should yearn for joy rather than happiness.

A common perspective about joy is that it is a consistent emotion cultivated internally. It emanates from making peace with who you are, your way of being and why you are. On the other hand, happiness is usually externally triggered and is often based on other things, people, experiences, places, and thoughts.

> *You make known to me the path of life; you will fill me with joy in your presence, with eternal pleasures at your right hand.* (Psalm 16:11, NIV)

In the presence of the Lord, there is fullness of joy. We know this and yet, we seek after other things more fervently than we seek after Him. We find ourselves seeking Him only after everything else fails.

One who knows joy must have experienced it to recognize that what they see is not just fleeting. Also, such a person is delighted to have others, especially those close to them share in this internally cultivated experience. **Friedrich Nietzsche** once expressed that, "*rejoicing in our joy, not suffering over our* *suffering, makes someone a friend.*" Friends should rejoice in the joy of their friends.

Joy is not as transitory as happiness and as such when one finds it, they have time to look at the world through different lenses before finally coming to their own conclusion about their experiences as well as those around them. If you've found joy and the people around you are not able to connect with you on this level, chances are they have yet to experience this internal transformation.

Reflection

What about you? Are you searching for joy or are you content with mere happiness?

_____

_____

_____

_____

_____

_____

_____

DAY 12

OFFENSE

Jesus warns of offenses in Luke 17:1 where he cautioned his disciples stating *"it is impossible that no offenses should come."* For a Christian to excel in their God-given purpose, it is essential for them to be free from offense.

John Bevere proffers that, *"offense is rampant among Christians for lack of genuine love." Also,* 1 Corinthians 8:1 states that *"knowledge puffs up, but love edifies."* The worse part about this is, so many people have been ensnared in this deceptive trap called offense that they have begun to normalize it. Love then takes second place to our prideful feelings of being 'wronged' by others.

This may lead to accusations of manipulation and other unrighteous judgment which is contrary to God's will. God urges us to make righteous judgments. In John 7:24, Jesus said, *"do not judge according to appearance, but judge with righteous judgment."* You might wonder, what is righteous judgment? Again, Jesus answers us with the word of God. in John 5:30, Jesus spoke, saying, *"I can of Myself do nothing. As I hear, I judge; and My judgment is righteous because I do not seek My own will but the will of the Father who sent Me."*

People who are easily offended are usually far removed from God and therefore, from grace. They are accustomed to leaning to their own understanding and seldom acknowledge the will of God in their hearts. Saying is not the same as doing.

> *If your brother sins against you, go and tell him his fault, between you and him alone. If he listens to you, you have gained your brother. But if he does not listen, take one or two others along with you, that every charge may be established by the evidence of two or three witnesses. If he refuses to listen to them, tell it to the church. And if he refuses to listen even to the church, let him be to you as a Gentile and a tax collector.* (Matthew 18:15-17, ESV)

One of the things that we do when we feel that someone has offended us is, we begin to treat them differently. Other times, we tell people about the offense instead of directly addressing the apparent offender. Here, Matthew is entreating us to only tell the person who has caused the offense. You only call for witnesses if the person is not receptive to your concerns.

Interestingly, Matthew uses the word 'brother' which to me is quite appropriate. More often than not, it is the people who are closest to us, brother, sister, parents, and friends who are more likely to offend us. We tend to hold them to a higher standard so that when we feel wronged by them, it is harder to forgive. We say things like, I expected better for you or after everything I have done for you, how could you treat me this way. Indeed, many crimes of passion emanate from feelings of offense from loved ones.

> *When someone gives you offense, it doesn't mean you have to take it.* (Joyce Meyer)

We should be careful to control our responses to extraneous variables and situations. Likewise, you are responsible for how you respond to the way other people treat you. Taking offense can become such a distraction that you are thrown off course from the pursuit of your vision. This is why offense is such a deadly weapon.

Reflection

How do you deal with situations where you believe others
have offended you?

_____

_____

_____

_____

_____

DAY 13

STRENGTH

Only by contending with challenges that seem to be beyond your strength to handle at the moment you can grow more surely toward the stars. (Brian Tracy)

I imagine that when **Bishop T.D. Jakes** embarked on his journey as a preacher, he was not nearly as refined and knowledgeable as he is today. Yet, based on the magnitude of his endeavours; writer, preacher, speaker, among other accolades, it is evident that he has deliberately and arduously worked toward his 'stars'. It is a lazy man or woman who sits on the sidelines, a comfortable spectator and attributes luck to the accomplishments of such men as **Bishop T.D. Jakes.** The essence of one's fruitful existence is rooted in their ability to harness their inner strength and push beyond ordinary or expected limits. Remember, no one starts out knowing their inner strength from the door. This must be harnessed.

> *I pray that out of his glorious riches he may strengthen you with power through his Spirit in your inner being,* (Ephesians 3:16, NIV)

Clearly, Paul is telling us through his letter to the Ephesians that the inner man needs strength. When your spirit is strengthened, you receive the power to combat fear, adversities, and weaknesses. We need reinforcement in our moral and spiritual nature if we are to carry out the duties God has ordained. Also, to withstand temptations and to remain steadfast in holding the vision He has for our lives.

Greatness is not attained by pure human strength alone. As you harness your strength, remember it's your decision to trust in the Lord with all your heart that opens up the way for you to reach beyond your limits. In his letter, Paul asked God to allow the Ephesians, *to know the love that exceeds knowledge so they may become filled to the measure of all the fullness of God.* (Ephesians 3:19, NIV). I believe Paul had recognized that the basis of strength was embedded in one's ability to exercise the highest form of love, the *agape* love. In 1 Corinthians 13, we are given the various dimensions of love which essentially shows that love conquers all things. This is why real strength emanates from within and cannot be attributed to extraneous variables, though inevitably it affects the latter.

It is my own firm belief that the strength of the soul grows in proportion as you subdue the flesh. (Mahatma Gandhi)

We are constantly reminded through the word of the Lord that operating at our highest potential requires the subjugation of our flesh. If you focus on strengthening your soul, you expose yourself to connecting with your inner being. You might ask, how can I accomplish this? It is through the direct influence of the Holy Spirit that strength is developed.

How can you experience this? First, you have to be prepared to give way to the will of God, it is only then that you expose yourself to this possibility. In Luke 1, when the angel Gabriel visited Mary, she submitted to God's will and so allowed herself to be visited by the Holy Spirit. Mary, then a young inexperienced girl found strength unlike any we have seen to bear the responsibility of being the mother of the Messiah.

When we meet real tragedy in life, we can react in two ways - either by losing hope and falling into self-destructive habits or by using the challenge to find our inner strength... (Dalai Lama)

It is well established that adversity introduces a man to himself, **James Allen.** Therefore, it is not for us to succumb to the pressure when we are faced with adverse circumstances. Rather, we are well placed to find our inner strength.

Reflection

How are you seeking to harness your strength? Write down 5 ways you can improve your strategies used to leverage your strengths. Write down 5 individuals you believe can hold you accountable during your transition.

_____

_____

_____

_____

_____

_____

_____

DAY 14

BELIEVE

And without faith it is impossible to please him, for whoever would draw near to God must believe that he exists and that he rewards those who seek him. (Hebrew 11:6, ESV)

Elizabeth Elliot was a missionary who went to live among the indigenous Auca people in Ecuador. As a missionary, she felt obliged to go this extra mile even after this very same people had killed her young husband while he was on his missionary journey. Most people would think her crazy to have made such a decision. However, when you decide to walk in obedience in the fulfillment of God's purpose in your life, you must believe in going the extra mile to win souls for Christ.

In her testimony at the Urbana Mission in 1996, **Elizabeth Elliott** quoted her late husband who said, *"missionary service was the categorical imperative for his life, an unequivocal commitment to the will of God, let it cost what it may."* This must have been the moment of his stark realization that obedience is our responsibility. Any results emanating from that obedience, whether good or bad is our opportunity to learn and grow.

Therefore, we do not exercise our conviction based on a contingency plan that a specific result must be guaranteed. We simply take determined action, knowing that we do not control the outcome.

You can leverage the power of belief to your advantage if you so desire. However, for most people, this is easier said than done. As you go through life and its plethora of challenges, it is very easy to give up on your dreams while you endure this journey of survival.

> *I believe that God has put gifts and talents and ability on the inside of every one of us. When you develop that and you believe in yourself and you believe that you're a person of influence and a person of purpose, I believe you can rise up out of any situation.* (Joel Osteen**)**

Many people are not where they ought to be in life, not because of inability or fate but lack of will to do more than is required. You can either appreciate that successful people are often characterized by grit and determination, or you can attribute their success to sheer luck. Either way, you are responsible for putting life into your vision. The sooner you realize the active role played by believing in yourself and the possibilities for your dreams, the better will be your chances for success.

As soon as Jesus heard the word that was spoken, He said to the ruler of the synagogue, do not be afraid; only believe. (Mark 5:36, NKJV)

Mark was speaking about a situation where they had just announced to the ruler of the synagogue that his daughter had died. The person relaying the message asked him, why trouble the teacher further? It was then that Jesus implored the ruler to abandon fear for, belief. He later restored life to the young girl to the amazement of the people. Here, we see that belief is inextricably linked to faith. You cannot believe in the possibility of your vision coming to fruition unless you have faith. And, what is faith?

Faith is the substance of things hoped for, the evidence of things not seen. (Hebrews 11:1)

Though the thing you are believing God for has not yet materialized on the physical plane, you have a knowing that it is possible. Even then, there are simply no guarantees in life. Personally, I think if there were, people in their heightened nature of power and control would inevitably disturb the order of things daily. Incidentally, this could potentially be more chaotic than it is presently. Abuse of others could become rampant.

Belief is something which, to take effect, must be embedded in the heart. **Roy T. Bennet** entreats you to, *"believe in your heart that you're meant to live a life full of passion, purpose, magic, and miracles."* Yet you realize that when you purpose in your heart to realize the big vision which God has placed there; it propels you into action.

One thing I have realized is individuals are not inclined to take purposeful action unless there is a conviction about what they are seeking to achieve. This conviction stems from their belief that it is possible or that it is necessary.

Reflection

Do you believe you can achieve whatever you put your mind to? How have you been exercising your convictions on a daily basis?

_____

_____

_____

_____

_____

DAY 15

DREAM

For about thirteen years he was a visible spokesperson and activist for the civil rights movement seeking to end racial discrimination and attain equality in the United States. In many ways, he was a visionary who envisaged things he scarcely saw while he lived, but came into fruition long after he exited this dimension in 1968. His name is **Martin Luther King Jr.** and today we honor his memory. Mr. King was also a Christian Minister who clearly believed in the operations of the all-encompassing power of God when we do His will. This is reflected in his infamous *'Mountaintop Speech'* given on April 3, 1968. He said,

> *Like anybody, I would like to live a long life. Longevity has its place. But I'm not concerned about that now. I just want to do God's will. And He's allowed me to go up to the*

mountain. And I've looked over. And I've seen the promised land. I may not get there with you. But I want you to know tonight, that we, as a people, will get to the promised land. (Martin Luther King Jr.)

He had faith that God's promise to his people would achieve completion. When you embark on a journey to realize a big dream, it is not because you have everything aligned to guarantee its completion. Rather, it is because you trust your process. More importantly, you trust in the will of God. If you are not there yet, I encourage you to seek Him because through Him you will find what you need to hold on to that dream.

Every great dream begins with a dreamer. Always remember, you have within you the strength, the patience, and the passion to reach for the stars to change the world. (Harriet Tubman)

You may have a desire to change the world and if so, you are definitely a dreamer. But, the absence of the tools required to effect such change may discourage you. Life is like that and it doesn't matter how many times we are told, *'you can do all things through Christ who gives you strength'* (Philippians 4:13), we tend to doubt our abilities. Let's face it, the fact that you allow yourself to dream doesn't mean you will not encounter some setbacks and disappointments. However, you should not let those inevitabilities catapult you into inaction. Keep on dreaming even if others call you crazy!

For we are God's handiwork, created in Christ Jesus to do good works, which God prepared in advance for us to do. (Ephesians 2:10, NIV)

When people say you are destined for greatness, it is because they know you were created for it. Understand that Christ created us in His likeness with the innate ability to do good works and to effect positive change in the world. Yet, so many of us are living beneath our God-given potential. I would like to think this is what marks the difference between those who are God-realized and those who aren't. When you become God-realized, you connect spiritually with our creator, God, and you realize that we are 'god' in manifestation and so nothing is impossible with Him. In recognizing your God-given abilities, you allow yourself to dream and then take massive action. You are meant for greatness! You are meant for more!

Reflection

What are your big dreams? What will you do to move into the
realm of dreaming big and seeing beyond your circumstances?

_____

_____

_____

_____

_____

DAY 16

WISDOM

How many of you have limited yourselves and the possibilities for your dreams because of the negative story you believe about yourself? Whatever you believe about your abilities eventually becomes you. If the story you believe is a negative one which presents you as small and insignificant, then you become small and insignificant in the eyes of the world. This doesn't happen because that is your fate, it happens because you have magnified those elements. As **Earl Nightingale** states in <u>The Strangest Secret</u>, *"you become what you think about all day long."*

But what if there was something which could over time change the negative stories you believe about yourself? What is the source of this phenomenon? That 'something' is WISDOM. Wisdom comes from God, *"If any of you lacks wisdom, let him ask God, who gives generously to all without reproach, and it will be given him."* (James 1:5, ESV). You must ask God for what you want. Wisdom allows you to walk in the way of the Lord. It inevitably operates to rewire and transform your mindset. This is not ordinary wisdom, but divine wisdom which emanates from 'Source' (God).

Spiritual wisdom dictates that what you don't wish to manifest in your life, you will not give power to. Negative non-affirming relationships, ideas, and beliefs about yourself are crippling. Proverbs 4 urges us to get wisdom at any cost. If someone tells you to believe positive things about yourself and the possibilities for your dreams, this may well be wisdom speaking, but you may never know if you have no sense of who she is. When Solomon had the opportunity to ask God for anything he wanted, he asked for wisdom and knowledge.

> *Because this was in your heart, and you have not asked riches or wealth or honor or the life of your enemies, nor have you asked long life—but have asked wisdom and knowledge for yourself, that you may judge My people over whom I have made you king— wisdom and knowledge are granted to you; and I will give you riches and wealth and honor, such as none of the*

kings have had who were before you, nor shall any after you have the like. (2 Chronicles 1:11-12, NKJV).

From the story of Solomon, we surmise that wisdom is not simply knowledge but the insight into how to effectively apply your knowledge. Wisdom, therefore, incorporates sagacity and understanding of how to conceptualize knowledge. In Proverbs 4:7 we are told that *"wisdom is the principal thing; Therefore, get wisdom. And in all your getting, get understanding."* Spiritual wisdom consists of a set of attributes that are deliberately shaped into practical skills about living God's way. The scripture places wisdom at the fore of everything suggesting it is a supreme godly attribute which we must all seek after if we are to live according to God's will.

> *The most important thing we can pray about for others is that they will know God better and that He will help them understand His will, grow in spiritual wisdom, and live lives that honor Him. We can pray that they will become more like Him and bear the fruit of His Spirit. (Stormie Omartian)*

So many times, we meet people going through adverse circumstances who ask us to pray for them. Some of them are our close friends, relatives or even brothers and sisters in

Christ. Yet, what does it mean to pray for them? Do we pray that their troubles will go away or that they will be strong in the midst of adversity? Both of those would be great prayers, but what happens when there is a recurrence? Do we pray the same prayers over and over again? I find that it would be more effective if instead, we pray that these individuals will advance in spiritual wisdom. I believe this will open the eyes of their understanding and allow them to live their lives on God's terms rather than theirs.

Let us pray

Heavenly Father, I pray that you will teach me to use the wisdom with which you have blessed me. Help me to use wisdom in all my endeavours. Let me see and treat wisdom as the principal thing. Thank you, Lord. In Jesus' name, I pray. Amen.

DAY 17

TRANSITION

If you do what you've always done, you'll get what you've always gotten Tony Robbins

Doing things, the same way every day will almost always yield the expected results. The problem is, though we often fancy the idea of a meaningful change, we are reluctant to get uncomfortable.

Today I urge you to start viewing transition as a natural part of your existence. Aside from the fact that we ordinarily make transitions from one job to another, from one home to another and even one educational institution to another, there is another form of transition which we should expect to make. This is a form of shift that is necessary for our individual uplift.

Truly, I say to you, unless you turn and become like children, you will never enter the kingdom of heaven. (Matthew 18:3, ESV).

Turning here means diverting your attention from temporal things and outward pleasures and vain precepts of honour and riches. This is not to be misunderstood as a glorification of poverty because there is little dignity in being poor. God has promised us abundance in all areas of our lives. However, you must be willing to redirect your attention to God in order to reap the harvest he has promised.

It doesn't matter where you are, you are nowhere compared to where you can go. (Bob Proctor)

One thing we know about children is, they have a natural tendency to be humble. They are not taken with superiority, pre-eminence and the need to feel special or better than others. These are all potential blockages to one's ability to make a transition from ordinary to extraordinary. A willingness to become uncomfortable with mediocrity can operate to catapult us into great territories that we have only dreamed of.

But the meek shall inherit the earth; and shall delight themselves in the abundance of peace. (Psalm 37:11)

Today, a friend reminded me that when we are transitioning to a new season in our lives, the people and situations that no longer fit will fall away. One of the things I have found that keeps people in a comfortable position is, we are afraid of letting go of things that do not serve us. It does not matter how many times we are reminded that change is inevitable, we are scarcely comfortable with it. Hence, anything which requires us to exit the comfort zone and do that which we have never done scares us, sometimes into inaction. This mindset has kept many talented people in a state of stagnation.

Isaiah reminds us to, *"remember not the former things, nor consider the things of old. Behold, I am doing a new thing; now it springs forth, do you not perceive it? I will make a way in the wilderness and rivers in the desert.* (Isaiah 43:18-19, ESV

Through this scripture, the prophet is also showing us that God will make a way even when it seems like there is no way. Imagine rivers in the desert, that is as unlikely as a camel going through the eye of a needle. (Luke 18:25). Yet, we are told that he certainly will make this possible if we can perceive that he wants to do a new thing in our lives.

When we open ourselves to be renewed by God, He will make a way for us.

Let us pray

Eternal Father, thank you for your insight and your grace. Today, I ask you to open the eyes of my understanding and permit me to work through my fears. I have a strong desire to change my life and I know that only you can make this possible. I submit myself to you oh Lord. Thank you for renewing my mind so I can see that change is necessary for me to grow spiritually. Thank you, Lord. In Jesus' name, I pray. Amen.

DAY 18

BROKENNESS

One of my favourite books is <u>A Return to Love</u> by **Marianne Williamson**. Every time I listen to her story of how she transitioned from loss and depression to a sense of knowing that there is a God who created the universe, I am in awe. Here's a woman who was born into Judaism and at some point, became disconnected from religion altogether. Her concerns were with philosophy and frantic rebellion. In her exploration, she discovered 'free will' which led her to her ultimate discovery concerning love. Our primary purpose on earth is to love and to be loved.

Brokenness involves removing inappropriate pride and self-reliance and building healthy God-reliance. (John C. Maxwell)

As Williamson studied the operations of God, she became enthralled by the simple yet profound impact of 'brokenness'. A former rebellious young lady with a proclivity to be prideful and self-indulgent was now being told to surrender everything to the will of God. Yet she found this was where she experienced freedom?

> *These are the ones I look on with favor: those who are humble and contrite in spirit, and who tremble at my word.* (Isaiah 66:2, NIV).

What about you? Would you love to experience brokenness in the sight of God?

To know God, we must come to Him with sincerity and penitence. A man or woman who wants to walk in the way of the Lord does not seek to justify their actions or ineptitude when they fall short of His glory. Instead, they seek to repent and submit to His will. This is the type of surrender God looks for from us.

Atonement is a good indication of brokenness in the site of the Lord. Psalm 51:17 tells us that *"the sacrifices of God are a broken spirit, A broken and a contrite heart— These, O God, you will not despise."* David was pointing out that God is not looking for burnt offerings and tangible sacrifices from us. Instead, he is looking for a heart that is repentant and broken in love.

To be broken in the sight of God means to be torn in your spirit over sin. It means you have reached the point of confession and acceptance of your wrong-doing. Hence, 'a broken spirit'. It takes someone who loves completely to be broken before God.

Prophet Frank Udoh who is the head of Christ Peace Ministries in Queens New York shared with his congregation what it means to love completely. He stated that for a believer to operate in the fullness of love, they must assess themselves for love's four dimensions, namely; length, breadth, depth, and height. These dimensions encompass how much passion we have in loving each other and whether we practice loving sacrificially. This takes us back to a vision of love as giving sacrificially to those around us by being broken in the face of sin?

Let us pray

Father, teach me how to become broken before you. Tell me what I must do the repent of my sins and sacrifice everything to your will. I want to be of service to you Lord. Use me for the building of your kingdom and for your ultimate glory. Thank you, Lord. In Jesus' name, I pray. Amen.

DAY 19

FORTRESS

A fortress is a person or thing not vulnerable to external influence or disturbance. When you have such reinforcement and protection around you, you feel secure. Most people would probably love to have a lifetime citadel to protect them, especially in adverse situations. Yet, no matter how many times we are told that we can have such access, we keep looking elsewhere.

> *A mighty fortress is our God, a bulwark never failing: our helper He amid the flood of mortal ills prevailing.* (Martin Luther)

In the game 'Who wants to be a Millionaire,' the player gets three lifelines. The lifelines they receive serve as support throughout the game. In the event the player meets up on a question that they have difficulty answering, they can use one of their lifelines. They have the opportunity to; phone a friend, ask the audience or split their four multiple-choice answers 50:50. The interesting about this game is, in most instances the lifelines run out before the player has the ability to win a million dollars.

> *Truly he is my rock and my salvation; he is my fortress; I will not be shaken.* (Psalm 62:6, NIV)

What if I tell you that you have access to a lifeline that will never run out? God is our bastion of protection and whenever we need Him, He is available to us.

> *The LORD Almighty is with us; the God of Jacob is our fortress.* (Psalm 46:7, NIV).

Unfortunately, we often take the long route when looking for solutions to our problems. Like the player in the game, when we face challenges, we have a tendency to ask our friends for advice. While it is good to have supportive relationships, more often than not, our friends can only offer a temporary solution.

I took my troubles to the LORD; *I cried out to him, and he answered my prayer.* (Psalm 120:1)

Going to God in prayer and submission opens up the way for us to enter His secret place where we can abide under His protection. (Psalm 91:1)

In John 16:33, Jesus tells us that he may have peace in Him. He expresses that here on earth we will have many trials and sorrows, but He has overcome the world. Therefore, we can rest assured that he is adept at addressing all our needs.

There are times when we may resort to asking anyone who is willing to listen, much like asking the audience in the game. Most of those people we ask can only offer their opinions or guesses about what they think might work for you. Knowing that you have an all-encompassing power about you who is ready to preserve and protect you is all the reassurance we need. Isaiah 41:10 entreats is to, have no fear as God is with us. Through the prophet Isaiah, He tells us, *"…be not dismayed, for I am your God. I will strengthen you, Yes, I will help you, I will uphold you with My righteous right hand."* (Isaiah 41:10, NKJV)

As you go through your day, remember you have a God who never fails. He will strengthen you in your time of distress, he will protect in his loving arms.

Let us pray

Heavenly Father, I look to you for comfort in my time of distress. Hear my cry and help me to always seek you in everything I do. Thank you for being my rock and my fortress. I know I can trust you. Thank you for your divine protection as I wade through these troubled waters. Thank you, Lord. In Jesus' name, I pray. Amen.

DAY 20

DESTINY

Know that as a Christian, your destiny is to be Christ-like in all of your ways. (Joyce Meyer)

When one learns to appreciate this position, they realize that every day they choose to become more like Christ, they are effectively living out their destiny.

"Destined for greatness," is a popular term we often hear from individuals who are self-motivated and determined. Many people believe they have the potential to achieve their idea of success while they live. As for me, *"I want to rule my destiny,"* (Buju Banton).

Many people, especially Christians may be taken aback by this choice of reference. However, for those who have listened to conscious lyrics for a long time, you know many songs sung by such artistes are based on biblical principles.

In 1997, Buju released a song called 'Destiny'. In the first verse, he states that *"the rich man's wealth is in the city, destruction of the poor is poverty."* This is a quote taken from **Proverbs 10:15**. A rich person feels secure because of their wealth, meanwhile the poor easily come to ruin because of their poverty. What if you decide to take control of your destiny and get on your way to success? While you ponder on this, remember, there is no honour in poverty.

> *Before I formed you in the womb I knew you before you were born I set you apart; I appointed you as a prophet to the nations.* (Jeremiah 1:5, NIV)

As with the prophet Jeremiah, God knew you before you were formed in your mother's womb. He has ordained you for greatness because as he states in John 15, you did not choose Him, He chose you and ordained you. One who is ordained is surely destined for greatness. You have the capacity to achieve whatever you desire. Never stop believing that. Embrace all of You, you are complete in the sight of God! You were created in His image and likeness!

God will not allow any person to keep you from your destiny. They may be bigger, stronger, or more powerful, but God knows how to shift things around and get you to where you're supposed to be. (Joel Osteen)

Sometimes, we know what it is that God has called us to do and yet we allow other people to stand in the way of our calling. Remember, though God has given us free will, it does not mean we can establish the curriculum. The curriculum was set from the time He chose and ordained us. Free will allows us to choose whether we will walk into that calling and so fulfill our destiny. I believe once one decides to start living a purpose-driven life, God will not allow anyone to keep them from their destiny.

Reflection

Do you believe you can control your destiny? How can you ensure you live your life with purpose on a daily basis?

_____

_____

_____

_____

DAY 21

BETRAYAL

One of the most well-known stories about betrayal found in the Bible is that of Judas Iscariot, one of Jesus' disciples. As we know, a disciple as mentioned in the gospels and the book of Acts, was a follower of Jesus. However, Judas was one of the twelve whom Jesus prayed to God about in **Luke 6:12.** We could easily conclude that he was one of the chosen, much like a close personal friend.

Historically, a disciple is a follower or adherent of a teacher. Such a person can be likened to a friend who is someone with whom you have a bond or mutual affection. You love, trust and respect your friends and this is reciprocated. Therefore, when there is betrayal, the hurt is intensified by the heightened expectation stemming from your friendship. I have found that this makes it extremely difficult to forgive such a person. Equally difficult is one's willingness to apologize after they have wronged you.

> *Then Judas, which had betrayed him, when he saw that he was condemned, repented himself, and brought again the thirty pieces of silver to the chief priests and elders, Saying, I have sinned in that I have betrayed the innocent blood. And they said, what is that to us?* (Matthew 27:3-4)

Yet, even Judas, after the betrayal of his friend, was repentant and tried to return the payment he had received. When he attempted to return the thirty pieces of silver to the priests and elders, they asked him an interesting question, 'what is this to us'? Likewise, when you betray your friend, no one else is there to help you atone for your disloyalty. It is a task which you must face alone.

Worse yet, you have no control over how they will respond to any attempt at apology or atonement. So, you must live with the possibility that they may never forgive you for the betrayal. Even so, you must do this so you can be free to move on with your life without the added encumbrance.

Naturally, when one makes progressive steps, there may be some who see it as a betrayal of their goals and interests. (Louis Farrakhan)

There is another dimension to this betrayal though. There are times when you seek to advance yourself and those you call friends, who may have taken permanent residency in their comfort zone, may somehow feel betrayed. This is not what we are concerned with. Never allow anyone to stop you from transforming your life. Any friend who seeks to impose guilt on you for trying is not a friend but is, in fact, a traitor.

Woe to you, destroyer, you who have not been destroyed! Woe to you, betrayer, you who have not been betrayed! When you stop destroying, you will be destroyed; when you stop betraying, you will be betrayed. (Isaiah 33:1, NIV)

Today, I urge you to be mindful of those who treat you as though you have betrayed them simply because you have chosen to answer God's call for your life. Many who call themselves friends will inhibit your progress by making you feel guilty about God's call to purpose. You must learn to differentiate what amounts to betrayal from flagrant manipulation and deception.

Reflection

Have you ever felt betrayed by someone you saw as your friend? Have you ever betrayed a personal friend? How can you avoid betrayal as you seek to answer God's call on your life?

_____

_____

_____

_____

_____

DAY 22

ACCESS

In whom we have boldness and access with confidence through faith in Him. (Ephesians 3:12, NKJV)

Historically, boldness, as used here, referred to freedom of speech. Paul was telling the Ephesians that we all have the autonomy to enter into the presence of God with confidence. God grants us the freedom to approach Him without hindrance or fear. We can take courage in knowing that God will come to our rescue in our various situations because of access to His sovereign care.

Dr. Wayne Dyer once said, *"meditation is a vital practice to access conscious contact with your highest self."* To me, this means, we must deliberately carve out time to spend meditating on the word of God. Remember, as stated in **Psalms 91:1** if we dwell in

Elohim's secret place, we get to abide under His precious protection. To reach your spiritual zenith, you must make a conscious and determined effort to spend time with God in quietude.

No one attains greatness by default. Greatness is attained by commitment and dedication. (Prophet Frank Udoh)

Where you reach in your spiritual journey is dependent on your lifestyle and commitment to God's instructions concerning your life. Recently, I was reminded that in the 'school of God' both the learned and the unlearned are as little children. We must be educated about how God wants us to govern our lives. This is what will grant us access to our divine calling.

A great door and effectual is opened unto me, and there are many adversaries. (1 Corinthians 16:9)

The fact that you have access to what God has planned for you does not mean you will enter without opposition and challenges. Therefore, while it is true that there is an opening or a door, that is not enough unless you can access it. Until you address the adversaries, until you deal with the problems at your door's entrance, you cannot enter. You will soon find that you can't subdue your adversaries unless you go through Jesus Christ.

> *I am the door. If anyone enters by Me, he will be saved, and will go in and out and find pasture.* (John 10:9, NKJV)

When you enter the door through Jesus, you receive your salvation. Only then will you be sufficiently armored to overcome your adversaries. The strength you find in Him will help you win the fight. Remember, you have access, but you must fight for it.

In life you will find that when your problems arise, you may even readily identify solutions and yet because of the challenges therein, you are not able to apply those solutions. This means you have to address the enemy within before you can solve the problems.

> *But as it is written, Eye hath not seen, nor ear heard, neither have entered into the heart of man, the things which God hath prepared for them that love him.* (1 Corinthians 2:9)

Paul is saying there has been no account of anyone having fully perceived and understood the value and splendor of the things God has prepared for us. Paul seems to be talking about a zenith of joy no human has ever conceived of. But, when you fully appreciate that Jesus died for the atonement of our sins and you make a conscious decision to repent and water your seed of faith, then you can experience a semblance of this joy God has prepared for us.

Reflection

What has been hindering you from accessing the door which God has opened for you? Write down the steps that you will take to remove these hindrances. What will you do first? Act Now

_____

_____

_____

_____

_____

_____

_____

DAY 23

SEED

When I was growing up, my father did Farming for a living. I found it to be the most fascinating thing as I watched the seeds come to life after just a matter of weeks in some instances. I used to marvel at what appeared to be thousands of miraculous moments. As much as I disliked the feeling of itchy weeds and wet grass against my skin whenever I went on the farm, I continued to be completely enthralled by the magnificence of life that could emanate from a small, seemingly insignificant seed.

A little seedling has treeness in it when it is put into the ground. You can't see treeness, you can't see the tree, yet you know it is in there. (Dr. Wayne Dyer).

Just as the seed which you see now, but which we know has a magnificent existence waiting to come to life for the world to see, you have greatness embedded within you. With the right nurturing your greatness will be manifested. You are a seed and when you focus on that divine power which we cannot see, but which we know flows through you, your greatness begins to take root.

> *The field is the world; the good seed are the children of the kingdom; but the tares are the children of the wicked one;* (Matthew 13:38)

Matthew pointed out that we are the good seed who will inherit the kingdom of God. We were adopted by God and are therefore heirs to His kingdom. But this does not occur as a matter of right. Just like a seed planted in good soil must be watered to germinate you must water your soul with the word of God.

> *The Spirit himself bears witness with our spirit that we are children of God, and if children, then heirs—heirs of God and fellow heirs with Christ, provided we suffer with him in order that we may also be glorified with him.* (Romans 8:16-17, ESV).

As seeds, we are sent into the world, as the apostles were then sent, to preach the gospel of Jesus Christ. The 'treeness' inside of us is waiting to come forth as we nurture our spiritual being. Know that in the process, you will face a multiplicity of adversities, you will suffer as Christ suffered, but in the end, you will reap the rewards of your labour.

> *You were designed for accomplishment, engineered for success, and endowed with the seeds of greatness.* (Zig Ziglar)

God created us all to thrive, to grow and to succeed. One of the greatest obstacles to our realizing our greatness is self-imposed doubt and fear. It is well established that you were endowed with the seeds of greatness, yet so many die with their music still inside because of the crippling effects of fear. That is not the destiny that God wants for His heirs. How can you be the heir of the highest King and still not live a life of abundance? Why sit on the sidelines and ask, who am I that the highest King should find favour with me? I will tell you why. You ask this question because you are seeing yourself only as a body and a body alone is a limited form of existence. However, you are not just a body, but a spirit encapsulated inside a body. Romans 8:16 already tells us that *"the Spirit himself bears witness with our spirit that we are children of God."* (ESV). Just as God is a Spirit, we too who were created in His image and likeness are spirits. When you begin to realize this, your eyes will open to the divine intelligence flowing within you. You will begin to manifest your greatness NOW!

Reflection

How can you begin to nurture the seeds of greatness which have been planted within you?

_____

_____

_____

_____

_____

DAY 24

ENDURANCE

A leader, once convinced that a particular course of action is the right one, must be undaunted when the going gets tough.
(Ronald Reagan)

I remember receiving a prophesy over two years ago and being told that in order for me to step into its manifestation, there were some things I would have to change. I was told I have to decide to part ways with the compromising of God's will concerning my life so as to walk into the calling which God has placed before me. For me, this was a true test of endurance as it meant I had to mentally assess my every move so has not to be disobedient to God's will. It was only when I began to watch my thoughts, my actions, and my reactions, that I was able to move away from compromise. As you can imagine, this has proven to be a long and arduous task. Yet, when we seek to perfect our craft in endurance, we no longer suffer from a mindset of lack, but one of abundance.

But let patience have her perfect work, that ye may be perfect and entire, wanting nothing. (James 1:4)

Every four years, at the Olympics, the world gets to see the unmatched endurance of the distance runners from countries such as ad Kenya and Ethiopia. Who can forget the remarkable abilities of Mo Farah of the United Kingdom? It is always amazing how these men and women can run for miles without giving up even when it seems like they have used up the last of their strength. That is what endurance is about. You continue to fight until you complete what you have started. Even in the midst of adversity, you press on to completion, knowing your reward is sure.

A man on a thousand-mile walk has to forget his goal and say to himself every morning, 'Today I'm going to cover twenty-five miles and then rest up and sleep. (Leo Tolstoy)

One way that I have been able to complete many difficult races is to break them up into small pieces and then take them one day at a time. It is the same way when you are pursuing your goals. You cannot focus so much on the overarching outcome that you forget to live through the small moments between.

When you make the end goal your overarching focus, things can easily become daunting to the point where you may get so overwhelmed, you are forced to abandon your journey prematurely. My suggestion to you is, break it up into small pieces and then focus on what you have to do today.

> *You need to persevere so that when you have done the will of God, you will receive what he has promised.* (Hebrews 10:36, NIV)

Your spiritual journey is one of endurance and unless you are mentally prepared to persevere during the difficult times, which are inevitable, you will miss out on His promise to give you an expected end. (Jeremiah 29:11)

> *Endurance is patience concentrated.* (Thomas Carlyle)

Reflection

How can one truly expect to endure unless they also exercise patience? It follows that if you have little patience, it is not likely that you will survive the difficulties of life. You have the ability to endure, the question is, how much do you want what you seek after?

_____

_____

_____

_____

_____

DAY 25

GIVING

Growing up in a linear society, we are taught by our parents to become go-getters. We cannot blame them for this, after all, they simply taught us what they themselves were told was the only way. Hence, you are practically coerced into going to school to GET and education, then you are taught to GET good grades so you can GET a scholarship or accolades or GET into a reputable tertiary institution. If you do well, this heightens your chances of GETTING a high paying job. After that, you are supposed to be well placed to GET some of the 'finer' [material] things in life.

In all things I have shown you that by working hard in this way we must help the weak and remember the words of the

Lord Jesus, how he himself said, 'It is more blessed to give than to receive. (Acts 20:35, ESV)

Even though people often remind us of the spiritual advantage of giving over receiving, ironically, most people are happier on the receiving end. It stands to reason that we often regurgitate feel-good statements, but fail to practice what we preach.

Then she arose with her daughters in law, that she might return from the country of Moab: for she had heard in the country of Moab how that the LORD had visited his people in giving them bread. (Ruth 1:6)

When Elimelech uprooted his family and went into the land of Moab, they were seeking to run away from the famine. They went to Moab believing they would have been able to survive owing to the availability of 'bread' there. However, what Naomi faced was the death of all the men in her family. Many people will not hesitate to go to a place where 'freebies' are being handed out, but when you call for volunteers for a good cause, the numbers often dwindle. For a while, the philosophy of getting things seemed worthwhile to me. It made sense until I realized all that I was instructed to go after

98

was only to set me up for attaining material possessions. This is why mental transformation is so crucial. Over time, as my mental purview changed, I began to appreciate that it is not getting which yields fulfillment in one's life but giving.

Instead of being a 'go-getter', I had to make the mental transition to become a 'go-giver'. In any event, the law of giving and receiving has long shown us that, *"giving opens the way for receiving."* (Florence Scovel Shinn)

Therefore, instead of going after the things of this world with frantic importunity, stop to see how you can give of yourself. Remember the word of God reminds us, *"every man shall give as he is able, according to the blessing of the LORD your God that he has given you."* (Deuteronomy 16:17, ESV).

> *Every day we have plenty of opportunities to get angry, stressed or offended. But what you're doing when you indulge these negative emotions is giving something outside yourself power over your happiness. You can choose to not let little things upset you.* (Joel Osteen)

If anger is inside of you, that is what you will give. **Dr. Wayne Dyer** has often reminded us that, *"you can't give what you don't* *have."* Therefore, if you do not possess love inside you, you are not capable of giving love. If you do not have peace, you cannot give peace or be peaceful. Giving is multidimensional and multifaceted. Hence, I urge you to give something today and remember the best things in life are free. Start with giving love!

Reflection

What can you give today? After reading this nugget, has your perspective on giving altered in any way? List at least five things that you can give to help make another person's life a little better.

_____

_____

_____

_____

_____

DAY 26

TIME

Can you relate to a situation where you were deeply hurt and desperately needed to share your pain with someone? I will confidently guess that you can. How about this; you share your pain with a friend, perhaps someone had wronged you and you felt like telling your friend about it, then they respond, *"time heals all wounds."* Apart from the fact that this is a clear misconception, to me such a brusque response only works to 'add fire to fury'. You might be better off trying to work through your pain on your own.

Roy T Bennett in his work, <u>The Light in the Heart</u> once said, *"time doesn't heal emotional pain, you need to learn how to let go."* I tend to agree with him. However, letting go of pain and suffering is easier said than done. Especially, when this pain was inflicted by someone you care about. Even so, you must learn to move beyond it. Otherwise, you run the risk of becoming stuck in hatred and resentment.

Scars have the strange power to remind us that our past is real.
(Cormac McCarthy)

Emotional pain can stay with you for years if you do not take the time to work through them. Even if the impact of what you feel subsides with time, every reminder of what happened is like being hurt all over again.

Psalm 34:18 tells us that, *"the LORD is close to the brokenhearted and saves those who are crushed in spirit."* This serves as an opportune reminder to those who are hurting, that God will help you work through your pain. It must be a relief to know that you don't have to go through it alone. Psalm 55:22 encourages us to, *"cast our burdens upon the LORD, and he will sustain us."*

Is time really the master of everything? Maybe not, but it is one of two things that are always constant, the other is change. It is also one of four things which will never come back, the others are; 'a spoken word, a neglected opportunity, and a sped arrow.'

> *As long as it is day, we must do the works of him who sent me. Night is coming, when no one can work,* (John 9:4).

A life passed cannot be regained, therefore use your time on earth wisely. Take time to intentionally do the will of God. Don't take anything for granted! You are meant for greatness!

Earl Nightingale postulates that the key reason why some people succeed and others do not is conformity. Most people spend their time doing what they are expected to do, without a thought for what they have the ability and authority to do.

He suggested that if you ask the average person, why do you work? They are likely to respond, 'everyone works. Have you no thought nor consideration for why YOU do it? Do you only work because everyone else does? What are you doing with the time you have here on earth? These are serious questions that I urge you to consider as you carry out the work of the Father as given specifically to you for you to do.

You are the master of your fate and what you do with your given time is completely up to you. Your time is valuable. Do not let anyone waste your time or distract you from your purpose.

Reflection

Are you spending quality time seeking the Lord? Are you being intentional about how you use your time? What can you do differently to make efficient use of your time?

_____

_____

_____

_____

_____

_____

_____

DAY 27

DISTRACTION

Distraction is simply interference with or shifting of one's focus from a thing of great importance to something less important. One of the most detrimental forms of distractions is being diverted from seeking God. We have a natural tendency to shift our focus to countless insignificant things that we erroneously magnify as being most important. The Bible refers to such distractions as idolatry.

> *Put to death, therefore, whatever belongs to your earthly nature: sexual immorality, impurity, lust, evil desires and greed, which is idolatry.* (Colossians 3:5, NIV)

When we become intentional about our pursuit of righteousness, things that currently consume our attention will fade away. God wants to use us for His glory and it is a travesty if we put worldly things before Him.

And this I speak for your own profit; not that I may cast a snare upon you, but for that which is comely, and that ye may attend upon the Lord without distraction. (1 Corinthians 7:35)

Today, it is very easy to get distracted from the pursuit of God's purpose for your life. We live in a world of technology and social media where many become consumed with the lives of others. We must begin to shift our focus to what really matters.

Wherefore I put thee in remembrance that thou stir up the gift of God, which is in thee by the putting on of my hands. For God hath not given us the spirit of fear; but of power, and of love, and of a sound mind. (2 Timothy 1:6-7)

A sound mind refers to self-control and self-discipline. God has blessed us with these significant abilities which if properly channeled will forcefully counteract distractions in our lives.

However, one has to be intentional about focusing on what drives purpose in order to become a success. This is what separates those who maximize their potential from those who do not. It is not so much about inherent gifts as against the lack thereof. However, if any and every minuscule and insignificant thing can get your attention, when they are compounded, you will find yourself behind on your dreams and your bills.

"You will never reach your destination if you stop and throw stones at every dog that barks." (Winston S. Churchill)

As God's purpose is being fulfilled in your life, you realize that many will not understand the operations of God. Not only that, but people will offer their unsolicited opinions about what they think is best for you or why what you are doing is bad for you. If you use valuable time to explain and defend your actions, you may never get to your destination.

It is very easy to become distracted by and engrossed with things outside of our purpose. Life is filled with adversities and challenges which can consume most of each waking moment of our lives.

I urge you to stay focused. Don't allow every whim on life's journey to attract your attention! Remember, you are destined for greatness.

Reflection

What distractions can you begin to remove from your life? What are some of the things that you can begin to move off your priority list?

_____

_____

_____

_____

_____

_____

DAY 28

DECEPTION

If you want to become fully mature in the Lord, you must learn to love truth. Otherwise, you will always leave open a door of deception for the enemy to take what is meant to be yours.
(Joyce Meyer)

Almost every day we have to contend with the imposter responsible for creating distrust in many great men and women. The worst part is, this *'Duke of Deception'* tends to rear his ugly head in the form of a family member or friend. Deception has ruined and continues to ruin many close relationships.

One of the most well-known occurrences of deception in the Bible comes to us in the story of twin brothers Esau and

Jacob. They were born out of the same womb and yet one deceived the other. Worse yet, the deception was orchestrated by their own mother.

In **Genesis 27: 1-40**, we are told about Isaac's intention to bless his older and favoured son, Esau. Isaac who was up in age and visually impaired called Esau and asked him to go into the field to *'catch game'* for food after which he would bless him. Little did he know that a household imposter, his wife Rebekah, was in earshot and was in that very moment planning her trickery.

> *Now Rebekah was listening when Isaac spoke to Esau his son. And Esau went to the field to hunt game and to bring it. So Rebekah spoke to Jacob her son, saying, indeed I heard your father speak to Esau your brother,"* (Genesis 27:5-6, NKJV)

Rebekah instructed her son Jacob to pose as Esau and deceive his father so he might receive the blessing intended for Esau. Not only did her plan work, but it also amounted to hostility between two brothers, something which took years to rectify. It is the same when we are hurt or deceived by those we love, we become consumed with hatred, fury, and animosity. We find it hard to forgive them and this just serves as a hindrance to our spiritual growth.

Be careful that you don't keep falling prey to deception. Be vigilant as there are many seeking to take advantage of those who are perceived as vulnerable. Remember, deception is nothing new. In the creation story, we see where the enemy used the serpent to deceive Eve and this was the outlet through which sin entered the world. The serpent is a well-known symbol of deception.

Behold, I give unto you power to tread on serpents and scorpions, and over all the power of the enemy: and nothing shall by any means hurt you. (Luke 10:19)

Also, when we are deceived, we open ourselves to yet another imposter, the bait of Satan called, 'offense'. But remember what Luke tells us in Luke 17:1 (NKJV), "*it is impossible that no offenses should come, but woe to him through whom they do come.*" Luke is also telling us that the person responsible for causing the offense will not go unpunished. However, when we become offended, we are also distracted from purposeful living.

Be careful that you do not fall into this trap of deception. *"Be sober, be vigilant; because your adversary the devil, as a roaring lion, walketh about, seeking whom he may devour."* (I Peter 5:8)

Reflection

What can you do differently to avoid falling into the trap of deception?

_____

_____

_____

_____

_____

_____

DAY 29

WEAKNESS

Have you ever gotten out of bed and felt like you weren't sure what to do next? You reviewed your long list of unfinished tasks and were further deterred from doing anything because it all seemed too overwhelming. You had to fight every urge to return to bed and hope that maybe you would feel better later. I cannot imagine that this is a unique experience understood by only a select few. It happens all too often to individuals I have interacted with.

So, what do you do, when 'doing nothing' seems like the most achievable option, when physical weakness threatens to get the better of you? I suggest you pray and ask God for the strength to rise above physical weakness and lethargy. This period of prayer is essentially a time of waiting on the Lord to revitalize you and replenish your strength.

> *But they that wait upon the LORD shall renew their strength; they shall mount up with wings as eagles; they shall run, and not be weary, and they shall walk, and not faint.* (Isaiah 40:31)

Many of us are plagued with impatience. This only operates to worsen any experience of overwhelm and lassitude. However, when we begin to understand that the LORD must be waited on for the manifestation of Himself in His perfect time, things start to shift in the direction of our dreams. Understand that the presence of God is worth waiting for as His promises are sure. He stated in Deuteronomy 31:6 that, *'He will never leave you nor forsake you'.*

Hold on to His promises and fight the good fight of faith. He will come through for you! He will strengthen you to withstand life's pressures. You cannot give up now!

Weakness is not always a physical thing. It may be something you are not good at. I urge you to be very careful with who you share your weaknesses. Some people can't wait for the opportunity to use them against you. There are some people in your life right now who are your enemies masquerading as friends. They dislike you and are lying in wait for your downfall. Even now, they are plotting how they may destroy you. Letting them know your weaknesses, makes you vulnerable to their devices.

> *Likewise the Spirit helps us in our weakness. For we do not know what to pray for as we ought, but the Spirit himself intercedes for us with groanings too deep for words.* (Romans 8:26, ESV)

Instead of sharing your weaknesses with untrustworthy friends, bring them to God. The Spirit will intercede on our behalf. God is your undeniable strength.

Reflection

What are some of your weaknesses? How can you turn them into strengths?

_____

_____

_____

_____

DAY 30

EMPOWERED

You are empowered to do the unimaginable. Jesus said in His Word, *"the Spirit of the Lord is upon me because he has anointed me to proclaim good news to the poor. He has sent me to proclaim liberty to the captives and recovering of sight to the blind, to set at liberty those who are oppressed,"* (Luke 4:8, ESV). In the same way, we are empowered through the Holy Spirit to do exploits for God's kingdom. Too many people are tiptoeing through life as if asserting their God-given power is not stronger than any fear tactics of Satan.

You are also empowered against the weapons of the enemy. (Luke 10:19). You may think me facetious for saying this, but nothing can hurt us unless we give it permission to do so. Faith comes by hearing and hearing and hearing and hurt comes from allowing and allowing. Until we see the power

God has given us, we are vulnerable to the weapons of the enemy.

> *Now to him who is able to do far more abundantly than all that we ask or think, according to the power at work within us,* (Ephesians 3:20, ESV)

The power at work within us is that of the Holy Spirit. When we realize the advantage afforded to us with this power and we begin to channel it, we become unstoppable. You then become equipped with the tools to fight against any challenges that you face. In 2 Corinthians 10:4, the LORD tells us that, '*the weapons of our warfare are not carnal, but mighty in God for pulling down strongholds'.* God has empowered us to overpower the seemingly more prevailing forces that seek to torment us. However, unless we decide to seek His face, we will not be sanctioned to fight the forces of darkness.

> *The LORD is my rock and my fortress and my deliverer, my God, my rock, in whom I take refuge, my shield, and the horn of my salvation, my stronghold.* (Psalm 18:2)

The interesting thing about this power we have been given is, it comes from God. It is impossible to tap into it unless you first become intentional about God's place in your life. Most people seek to exert power and control over others in order to make them feel less than. However, the power God gives us enables us to extend empowerment to others.

> *You were put on this earth to achieve your greatest self, to live out your purpose, and to do it courageously.* (Steve Maraboli)

In my work as a Personal Transformation Strategist, my primary goal is to make others feel empowered. I cannot imagine how it could help anyone if my goal was to gain and maintain power any control over another. That is characteristic of an abuser. The kind of power God gives us is rooted in love. We exert it only to empower and or protect others from harm. Anyone who uses their God-given power to do harm is not operating under the auspices of the Holy Spirit.

You have the power to take the reins in your life. Don't wait for permission from others. God has already given you the ultimate authority. He has given you a spirit of power, of love and a sound mind. (2 Timothy 1:7)

Reflection

Do you believe you could be better placed to achieve your goals if you felt empowered? What will you do to begin to channel your innate power?

_____

_____

_____

_____

_____

DAY 31

GRATITUDE

Every creature of God is good, and nothing is to be rejected, if it be received with thanksgiving: for it is sanctified through the word of God and prayer. (1 Timoth4 4:4-5, ASV)

Today as you go through your day, take the opportunity to say thank you. Gratitude embodies an all-encompassing quality of being thankful. It is of utmost importance to show appreciation and recognize kindness. Many will tell you that the law of attraction operates such that when you show kindness, you attract the same to you. Showing gratitude goes way beyond the law of attraction though. It is deeply embedded in God's manual which governs our lives, that is, the Bible. Psalm 69:30 states, *"I will praise God's name in song and glorify him with thanksgiving."* Even in worship, we must be thankful.

A friend once asked me, "why do you always seem so optimistic, like you have no problems?" My response was, *"I like to send positive energy into the universe."* But it is not the law of attraction which makes gratitude necessary, it is the unchanging love of God.

> *Let them give thanks to the LORD for his unfailing love and his wonderful deeds for mankind.* (Psalm 107:8, NIV)

Just be grateful that God created you inherently good. It means that even though sin defiles us, we have the opportunity to be saved by His unchanging grace. Be thankful that you have the chance to change your life, by changing the way you perceive yourself and the rest of the world. Do not base the way you treat others on their failure to be grateful for your good deeds. Rather, treat them with love and be grateful for the opportunity to learn from them.

> *I thank my God always concerning you for the grace of God which was given to you by Christ Jesus.* (1 Corinthians 1:4, NKJV)

Gratitude should not only be reserved for significant occurrences or experiences. I believe in developing a culture of expressing thanks. It is true that it becomes extremely difficult to harbor any thought of positivity when there are blaring obstacles hovering about you.

However, it is perhaps in such moments that it is most important to show gratitude. I can allude to a myriad of personal experiences whereby I had a grateful response to a difficult situation and the outcome was much better than I would have ever imagined.

> *Develop an attitude of gratitude, and give thanks for everything that happens, knowing that every step forward is a step toward achieving something better than your current situation.* (Brian Tracy)

Gratitude helps you to construe your situation in a more positive way. In fact, with gratitude, sometimes your mindset is so adjusted as to even allow you to find solutions to the very problem that you are experiencing. So, take a moment to say thank you for the things that are good in your life, even if the bad seems to outweigh the good presently. Develop an attitude of continuous gratitude.

Reflection

List at least five people and five things you are grateful for today.

_____

_____

_____

_____

_____

_____

_____

DAY 32

FORGIVENESS

Forgiveness encompasses compassion, understanding, and patience. Many have entreated us to forgive and forget. Yet others have said, 'I will forgive, but I won't forget'. Both mindsets clearly show us that to forgive is a challenge faced by most people and though we often commission each other to forgive, it is easier said than done. Even so, forgiveness is an integral part of our growth as kingdom warriors.

> *Get rid of all bitterness, rage and anger, brawling and slander, along with every form of malice. Be kind and compassionate to one another, forgiving each other, just as in Christ God forgave you."* (Ephesians 4:31-32, NIV).

The scripture is resolute about how we should govern our lives. It is not a suggestion that we should desist from harbouring thoughts of bitterness and anger, it is a directive. We are told in no uncertain terms that as a part of our daily living as Christians, we must do these things. The significant part of these instructions is the fact that despite all my sins; unforgiveness, anger, bitterness, malice and callousness, God has forgiven me. Why then should I find it hard to forgive others who have hurt me?

You can't forgive without loving. And I don't mean sentimentality. I don't mean mush. I mean having enough courage to stand up and say, I forgive, I'm finished with it. (Maya Angelou)

It seems to me that the difficulty we face with unforgiveness emanates from our lack of genuine love for each other. People lie and scheme and these things create distrust and sometimes a change in the love between people. Therefore, when it is time for us to forgive these same people, the difficulty intensifies because we don't know how to look past what they have done and see the fallible beings with the potential to right their wrong.

All we can see is the wrong that they have done and this turns into self-righteous judgment against them. But, Isaiah 53:6

states that we are all like sheep that have gone astray. We have turned to our own ways of doing things and yet God has laid our iniquities on Jesus Christ, instead of on us.

> *Forgiveness should start now. Putting off forgiving only deepens the wound. Clinging to bitterness postpones happiness. Life is short, time is fleeting. Today is the day to forgive.* (Wilfred Peterson)

If Jesus who was and is and is to come, has no sin, and yet he died for our transgressions, why can't we learn to love each other enough to forgive? Today, I entreat you to start your process of healing by forgiving the one who has wronged you the most!

When you decide to forgive, you are being obedient to God's instructions. Even the word of God tells us that obedience is better than sacrifice. 1 Samuel 15:22 tells us that, *"to obey is better than sacrifice, and to hearken than the fat of rams."* So, are you going to let your lack of forgiveness prevent you from walking in complete obedience? Or will you ask the Lord to teach you how to forgive so you can walk in His grace? Forgiveness marks the beginning of your healing process. Therefore, when you forgive, you are actually doing more for you than for the one who has wronged you.

Let us pray

Lord, teach me how to forgive those who have caused me pain and hurt. Help me to let go of the past hurt so I can experience true freedom. Cleanse me from unrighteousness. Help me to walk in the way of peace. Thank you, Lord. In Jesus' name, I pray. Amen.

DAY 33

OTHERS

When you seek happiness for yourself, it will always elude you.
When you seek happiness for others, you find it for yourself.
(Dr. Wayne Dyer)

It is not common for us to place the happiness of others before our own. Every so often you will hear someone say, 'I just want to be happy', and there is nothing wrong with that. However, if you take the spotlight off of yourself for just a moment to tune in to someone else's wellbeing, you may well find it gratifying to help that person find peace.

> *And if anyone gives even a cup of cold water to one of these little ones who is my disciple, truly I tell you, that person will certainly not lose their reward.* (Matthew 10:42, NIV)

There aren't many people who will show concern for or even move to help others when they themselves are experiencing hurt or despair. Yet, here we are entreated to shift our attention to someone who is 'naked' and in need of help. Not only that, but a person who does this act of selflessness has a certain reward. God does not want us to reject each other but embrace one another, despite our outward differences.

In his book Les Misérables, **Victor Hugo** proffers that, *"it is a charming quality of the happiness we inspire in others that, far from being diminished like a reflection, it comes back to us enhanced."* Not only will diverting our attention to making others happy enhance their wellbeing, but it will make greater our own happiness whether now or in the future.

> *Do nothing from rivalry or conceit, but in humility count others more significant than yourselves. Let each of you look not only to his own interests, but also to the interests of others.* (Philippians 2:3-4, ESV)

Personally, I believe one's zenith in life is the degree of their contribution to the lives of others. Many are plagued with perpetual bouts of unhappiness because they become engrossed in self-aggrandizement and self-preservation. As one who is prepared to Honour God, you must also be willing to put others before you. That is a true symbol of God's agape love.

> *"Each of us should please our neighbors for their good, to build them up. For even Christ did not please himself but, as it is written: "The insults of those who insult you have fallen on me."* (Romans 15:2-3, NIV)

As Isaiah 53 tells us, Christ was wounded for our transgressions and bruised for our iniquities. Loving others is characterized by this same level of selflessness. God wants us to love each other as much as we love ourselves or even more. Better yet, he wants us to exercise the same level of love God did when He sent His only son to die for our sins.

Reflection

Do you believe in putting others before you in any circumstances? If so, what acts of selflessness can you incorporate in your life to teach others about God's love for us?

_____

_____

_____

_____

_____

_____

DAY 34

ONENESS

But in fact, God has placed the parts in the body, every one of them, just as he wanted them to be. If they were all one part, where would the body be? As it is, there are many parts, but one body. (1. Corinthians 12:18-20, NIV)

There is an expectation from Kingdom builders that there will be an appreciation for unity and diversity in the body of Christ. Just as our bodies are made up of several organs, all performing different functions, so the body of Christ consists of people with different gifts. Therefore, our bodies cannot exist independently of our collective organs.

Likewise, in the body of Christ, believers are given different spiritual gifts according to the will of God. However, we all make up one body. Though we benefit from the spiritual gifts of our brothers and sisters, human beings have a proclivity to envy others because of their abilities. I urge you to be mindful of this. For the body of Christ to excel in oneness, we must be happy for each other despite our individual gifting. Besides, as Paul reminded the Corinthians, in 1 Corinthians 12, in the end, only love matters.

There are millions of stories where individuals were mistreated, ostracized or even killed by others because of the gifts given to them by God. People who subject others to such ills have not been enlightened to our state of oneness in God's sight. When we accept this oneness and understand that the spirit of God which flows through us is the same spirit that gives diverse gifts, we are lifted. We begin to operate at such a high frequency that loving others become the norm.

One God and Father of all, who is over all and through all and in all. (Ephesians 4:6, ESV)

We know that our Father in heaven is one God who manifested in the flesh and dwelled among us and now exists in the Spirit. The earth and everything in it belong to Him. As Psalm 24 states, *"the earth is the Lord's and the fullness thereof."* We too are part of God and were created in His image and likeness. Yet we fight each other and constantly seek to be better than the other person. Personally, I believe there are no 'betters', just different.

> *Then God said, "Let us make man in our image, after our likeness. And let them have dominion over the fish of the sea and over the birds of the heavens and over the livestock and over all the earth and over every creeping thing that creeps on the earth.* (Genesis 1:26, ESV)

Today, I urge you to see yourself as God sees you. See yourselves as part of His body designed to perform different functions, but of equal importance. In God's sight, we are one. He has given us different callings and mandates. However, the ultimate goal is to win souls for Christ so we can dwell together in eternity.

> *"I believe that Jesus realized His oneness with God and He showed, what He attempted to do was show the way to all of us, how to realize our own oneness with God also, so He's a precursor.* (Eckhart Tolle)

Since we were made in His image and likeness, to this extent, we are one with Him. God sees Himself in us. However, He has given us free will to choose the path of righteousness. Also, notice the LORD said, "let us make man," not men. This suggests that we all are one being, man, separated only my multiple human bodies.

Reflection

Do you believe that God sees His creation, man, as one? How can you show others that you do not see yourself as completely separate from them?

_____

_____

_____

_____

_____

DAY 35

RELAX

I've always associated relaxing with resigning, which somehow translates in my head to mean laziness. Therefore, whenever a friend would encourage me to 'just relax', I would become defensive. This may not make sense to you, but for someone who has always prided myself in doing something worthwhile with me time, relaxing has taken on a new meaning for me and over the years had lost its intended appeal. That is until I discovered the very brief Psalm 127.

Psalm 127: 2 states that *"it is vain for you to rise up early, to sit up late, to eat the bread of sorrows: for so he giveth his beloved sleep."* Rest is a gift from God. Therefore, it is completely impractical to dedicate every day to working from sunup to sundown, such that you forget to live and enjoy life right now.

Be mindful that you do not construe this as some sort of a movement against hard work. Like the author of <u>Grit</u>, **Angela Duckworth**, I am a major proponent of grit and determination. Yet, I've also learned that wisdom requires us to dedicate time for relaxation and rest.

> *Except the LORD build the house, they labour in vain that build it: except the LORD keep the city, the watchman waketh but in vain.* (Psalm 127:1)

Many people are going about their lives in a frantic way, dedicating time and effort to things God did not ordain. The Psalmist is reminding us that unless God ordains that which you seek after, your work may be done in vain. One of the benefits of relaxing is the opportunity to gain clarity of thought and vision. The ability to know if God has called you to do what you are doing.

> *What do people get for all the toil and anxious striving with which they labor under the sun? All their days their work is grief and pain; even at night their minds do not rest. This too is meaningless.* (Ecclesiastes 2:22-23, NIV)

It is pointless to work all day only to spend your night worrying over the work done or that set aside for tomorrow. If you do this, you find that you live to work and you work to live. This is not the life God has promised us. This sort of frantic striving prevents you from living in the Now.

In Luke 12:27, NKJV, we are urged to, *"Consider the lilies, how they grow: they neither toil nor spin; and yet I say to you, even Solomon in all his glory was not arrayed like one of these."*

Not only is this scripture telling us not to worry, but we also see that even when you take time to relax between work, God will still provide for you. Working is not only important, but it is necessary. However, relaxation is also a requirement.

There are many people who have suffered from heart attacks and nervous breakdowns because they did not take the time to relax along the way. Read a book, watch your thoughts, clear your mind! Relax!

Relax and rejuvenate your sacred-spirit. (Lailah Gifty Akita)

Reflection

How do you relax when things get really busy?

_____

_____

_____

_____

_____

DAY 36

ATTITUDE

A few years ago, a very talented young lady came to work under my supervision. One of the most noticeable things about her was how she responded to instructions or requests. When asked to complete a task or when a client needed her assistance or to just about every conceivable scenario, she always seemed ready and willing.

With her, you never tire of hearing words like, 'absolutely', 'certainly', 'my pleasure' and 'indeed'. I cannot count the number of times a fellow colleague would make snide remarks such as, 'I wonder what happy pill she took this morning' or 'what is she on today'? I too found myself at times being cynical about her attitude. After all, who could be that cheerful at all times? Then one day I came across this quote by **Dr. Wayne Dyer,**

Begin to change the vocabulary you use to describe yourself and your expectations. Instead of saying; If I'm lucky, Perhaps, and One never knows, use words and phrases like Absolutely, Certainly, and "I know I can." When you use words that reflect an absence of doubt, you will conduct your life in the same way.

It is amazing how you could spend your entire life being a certain way and then one single experience can alter your way of thinking forever. This position taken by Dr. Dyer marked a shift in my thought process and specifically, how I perceived the world and those in it.

I have come to the realization that attitude is everything. That young lady I mentioned did not take some type of happy pill. She simply chose to be buoyant and upbeat because these are variables, she had control over. Likewise, we should adopt a positive mental attitude and this will transcend into how we react to and treat others around us.

A joyful heart is good medicine, but a crushed spirit dries up the bones. (Proverbs 17:22, ESV)

Whatever is in one's heart protrudes outward. It means when we purpose in our hearts to be cheerful and positive, people begin to see us this way. Also, this operates to alter our perspectives about life and others around us.

> *Whatever you do, work at it with all your heart, as working for the Lord, not for human masters.* (Colossians 3:23, NIV)

When we focus on putting our all into what we do, it prevents us from becoming sidetracked by secondary activities. Do you remember the phrase we were taught in elementary school which states that *"whatever you do, do it well or not at all?"* This thought has stayed with me since I learned it and has allowed me to do my best in almost everything I do.

However, I had not really contextualized it in terms of attitude. At least, not until I met Dr. Dyer through his work. Now, I know that my attitude can change my life over time and as such I must be intentional about having a positive attitude. Also, my attitude can impact others as well as how I interact with others. Plus, as **John C. Maxwell** reminds us, *"people may hear your words, but they feel your attitude."*

Let us pray

Dear Lord, please help me to develop a positive mental attitude. Let me be intentional about my attitude towards other people in my daily interactions. Father, I know sometimes I can be impatient with others especially when they do things, I think are foolish. Help me to develop patience and seek only to make righteous judgments. Thank you, Lord. In Jesus' name, I pray. Amen.

DAY 37

HEALING

When we think of healing, we primarily associate it with physical healing. We consider it in terms of restoration of health from sickness or imbalance. Therefore, we seek to cure whatever ailment we suffer from using medication and for some, natural remedies. Even the New Testament is replete with instances of people seeking healing and being healed by Jesus and His disciples. Therefore, physical healing is extremely important and necessary. However, spiritual healing is also very important.

> *My wayward children, says the Lord, come back to me, and*
> *I will heal your wayward hearts.* (Jeremiah 3:22, NLT)

Here, God speaks of a different kind of healing, the healing of the heart. Human beings have the propensity to explore things with which they have an emotional connection. Whenever this happens and they are disappointed, they may experience broken hearts. This is especially common with human relationships, and so we seek to 'mend the broken heart' through counseling, therapy and for some, prayer. However, when God speaks of healing our wayward hearts, He is referring to the restoration of our faith in Him. Faith comes through intentional time with God.

The only work that will ultimately bring any good to any of us is the work of contributing to the healing of the world. (Marianne Williamson)

Consider this, even the world in which we live needs healing. Many times, when people state that they need a change, what they are really talking about is a mental transformation, a renewing of their minds. (Romans 12:2). It is not something as superficial as a change of scenery. If you don't believe me, when you get that feeling of longing, the gnawing need for a change, pack your bags, get up and jump on a plane to your favourite destination and see if the longing suddenly disappears. In more cases than not, it doesn't and so one keeps searching. Unfortunately, there are those who die, still searching.

> The LORD *will strengthen him upon the bed of languishing: thou wilt make all his bed in his sickness.* (Psalm 41:3)

Sometimes we have to look outside of ourselves and see what we can do to help others in their healing process. At times, these people may be the very ones who have caused you pain which means, you also need healing. However, as Marianne Williamson articulated, *"My self-healing lies in praying for those who have harmed me."* Praying for them does not mean, they have not hurt you. It simply means you need to heal yourself through your ever-fervent prayer.

> *Christ is the Good Physician. There is no disease He cannot heal; no sin He cannot remove; no trouble He cannot help. He is the Balm of Gilead, the Great Physician who has never yet failed to heal all the spiritual maladies of every soul that has come unto Him in faith and prayer.* (James H. Aughey)

Any form of healing we are looking for, God can and will provide it. We simply need to look to Him, the author and finisher of our faith. (Hebrews 12:2)

Reflection

Do you believe God can provide both spiritual and physical healing? What can you do differently to partake of His healing grace and power?

_____

_____

_____

_____

_____

DAY 38

GUILT

It is a hard thing to let go of the mistakes we've made and sins. God wants us to do that because He knows the guilt and the condemnation will keep us from becoming who He has created us to be. (Joel Osteen)

We have a tendency to judge others even for the slightest mistakes they make. If deemed judgmental, one is likely to be faced with much reproach from the hearers of such judgments. But, how many of us realize that we judge ourselves even more harshly? Like **Joel Osteen** says, human beings find it extremely difficult to let go of mistakes. We spend a lot of time pondering how differently we would have done things if we had the opportunity for a 'do-over'. Yet, how can we walk into God's purpose for our lives if we are inhibited by guilty feelings and feelings of remorse?

Dr. Wayne Dyer entreats us to, send guilt out of our lives by practicing to release this emotion and replacing it with love, kindness, and forgiveness. When you dwell on guilt over your past conduct, you are essentially inviting turmoil into your life. However, when you make a decision to avoid the particular conduct in the future and you commit to this, it will lead to your inevitable transformation. Rather than misusing your mental energy on something you cannot change, learn from it and grow from it. Guilt is a misuse of God's gift to you. *"For God hath not given us the spirit of fear; but of power, and of love, and of a sound mind."* (2 Timothy 1:7)

> *Let us draw near to God with a sincere heart and with the full assurance that faith brings, having our hearts sprinkled to cleanse us from a guilty conscience and having our bodies washed with pure water.* (Hebrews 10:22, NIV)

God called David, 'a man after My own heart' because David, though he sinned many times, had a repentant heart. When we draw near to God and we repent from our sinful ways, there is no need to invite guilt into our lives. God has offered us this wonderful opportunity of salvation through repentance, so why allow what you have done to keep you from who you can become in Christ?

> *I was tormented with guilt for years and years. In fact, it was so bad that if I didn't feel wrong, I didn't feel right!* (Joyce Meyer)

Some of us allow guilt to have such a profound impact on our conscience that it becomes a part of our way of life. Today, I urge you to separate yourself from guilt and shame and cleave to the offer of repentance and a fresh start that God has made available to you.

You cannot have a better past. You did what you thought was right or good at that time. Now, you have the opportunity to walk into a brighter future, to become a better you. grasp it! Too often, we go about life in a casual way as if tomorrow is promised to us, when we all know that it is not.

Let us pray

Lord, teach me how to send guilt out of my life. Teach me how to move on without this added baggage of remorse and regret. Show me how to start afresh today that I may find the fullness of joy in you. You are my rock and my fortress, show me how to look to you for support as I press on to my higher calling. Thank you, Lord. In Jesus' name. Amen.

DAY 39

PRAYER

Jesus' disciples had the opportunity to ask Him for anything, but they asked Him to teach them how to pray. (Luke 11:1) One can surmise that having been around Him for quite some time, they would have observed that Jesus spent a lot of time in prayerful reverence to God. Further, His prayers yielded results. *"The effectual fervent prayer of a righteous man availeth much."* (James 5:16)

Matthew 6 reminds us that prayer is not meant to be an open spectacle seeking to create the idea of your holiness in front of others. Instead, it should be an intimate supplication to God and your father who hears you in secret will reward you openly. (Matthew 6:5) Understand that it does not mean one cannot pray openly. Corporate prayer has proven to be very effective in the lives of believers. Moreover, *"...where two or three gathers in my name, there am I with them."* (Matthew 18:20, NIV)

> *"To gather with God's people in united adoration of the Father is as necessary to the Christian life as prayer."* (Martin Luther)

As much as God requires intimate time with him from all believers, uniting in prayer is an integral part of our development as kingdom builders. Also, there are no limits to what you can bring before God in prayer.

I strongly believe that if whatever you ask of God is not meant to be, He will reveal Himself through the Holy Spirit. But, in the book of Philippians, we are encouraged to pray about everything. Prayer is a conversation between you and God. Especially when you are seeking Him for something specific. Instead of becoming anxious because of your uncertainty, go to Him on your knees.

> *Do not be anxious about anything, but in every situation, by prayer and petition, with thanksgiving, present your requests to God. And the peace of God, which transcends all*

understanding, will guard your hearts and your minds in Christ Jesus." (Philippians 4:5-6, NIV)

Prayer is an effective tool to combat fear and worry. Especially since we have a tendency to worry about things which we believe will hurt us or go against our expectations. Here, we are reminded that when we make our requests known to God through prayer, He is faithful and just to grant them in His perfect timing.

Our prayers may be awkward. Our attempts may be feeble. But since the power of prayer is in the one who hears it and not in the one who says it, our prayers do make a difference. (Max Lucado)

Having an active prayer life is not about elocution and verbosity. God answers the prayers of the meek and unlearned as much as He does that of the wise and prudent. Here, we are being reminded that it is the one who hears our prayers, God, who is equipped to answer them. All He asks is that we come to Him in complete surrender.

This is the confidence we have in approaching God: that if we ask anything according to his will, he hears us. (1 John 5:14, NIV)

The Bible tells us that what we believe in our hearts is possible. Not only that, but there are no limits to what we can ask of God in prayer. Therefore, if you are feeling hopeless today or in this precise moment, take a deep breath and breathe a word of prayer.

Let us pray

Father, teach me how to stay connected to the anointing through prayer. I desire a robust prayer life and I am guided by your instructions about how I should pray. I am asking you to help me to stay focused on you as I work to develop an active prayer life. Thank you, Lord, for your blessings on me. In Jesus' name, I pray. Amen.

DAY 40

TRANSFORMATION

"Put to death, therefore, whatever belongs to your earthly nature: sexual immorality, impurity, lust, evil desires and greed, which is idolatry." (Colossians 3:5, NIV)

Most times when a believer speaks about transformation, they will reference Romans 12:2 which entreats us to be transformed by the renewing of our minds instead of conforming to the ways of the world. While this is a compelling reference, it is quite general and leaves the believer to surmise what 'things of the world' they should avoid or reject. But, when I read Colossians 3, it is clear that a prerequisite for total transformation is to die to self. The scripture implores us to put fleshly desires to death in order to advance in Christ. Also, in 2 Corinthians 5:17, we are told that, *"… if any man be in Christ, he is a new creature: old things are passed away; behold, all things are become new."* To truly be in Christ, we must extricate ourselves from the things that keep us weak and bounded. We must put old things away from us and start anew.

> *One can choose to go back toward safety or forward toward growth. Growth must be chosen again and again; fear must be overcome again and again.* (Abraham Maslow)

Some people fail to experience transformation because they are inhibited by fear. But I once read somewhere that 'fear' is just inverted faith. It means that the same amount of energy it takes to exercise fear can be channeled into exercising faith. It is all about the mindset, the inner transition from who you are to who you can become. The fact is, transformation is really a spiritual experience.

> *Transformation literally means going beyond your form.* (Wayne Dyer)

Dr. Dyer describes our form as the physical world in which we live along with the things in it that appeal to us. Our form is also our bodies. To transform our lives, we must, therefore, go beyond our flesh. We must go inward, go beyond, soar above the limits of our bodies and connect with our spirit.

> *And we all, who with unveiled faces contemplate the Lord's glory, are being transformed into his image with ever-increasing glory, which comes from the Lord, who is the Spirit.* (2 Corinthians 3:18, NIV)

When we receive salvation, the veil is removed from our hearts thus making us free to love and to be loved. Moreover, God's glory is the supernatural source for our spiritual transformation. Note that spiritual transformation protrudes from within, thus indicating that it is a process. This kind of deep-rooted change speaks to an alteration in our fundamental nature and character. Hence, as we transform, we become more like Him in whose image and likeness we were made. You have the ability to change your life, by changing the way you think and act as a believer.

In the book, Success Through a Positive Mental Attitude, **Napoleon Hill and W. Clement Stone** tell us that we operate with an invisible talisman. They proffer that on one side, of this talisman we have a positive mental attitude and on the other, a negative mental attitude. They believe it is up to us to use which one we will channel for our desired growth. A key part of your transformation requires a shift in mindset. You must decide what you want to change and then begin to do what is necessary to effect that change. Therefore, transformation starts from within and protrudes outward.

Let us pray

Father, thank you for reminding me that I can be transformed by renewing my mind. I long for a change in my life. I desire more than anything to live my life with purpose. Lord, help me to trust in you with all my heart and guide me so I will not lean to my own understanding. Thank you, Lord. In Jesus' name, I pray. Amen.

BIBLE VERSIONS

1. **King James Version**

2. English Standard Version (ESV)

3. New American Standard Version (NASB)

4. New International Version (NIV)

5. New King James Version (NKJV)

6. New Living Translation (NLT)

7. New Revised Standard Version (NRSV)

MAKE THE VISION PLAIN

"Write the vision, and make it plain upon tables, that he may run that readeth it."

Habakkuk 2:2)

Now that you are inspired to transform your life. It is time to get started. Use the space below to write down your vision and the steps you will take toward its realization. The scarier, the better. Right now, how you will do it is none of your business. Your only concern is to make the vision plain before you and God.

_____

_____

_____

_____

_____

_____

_____

_____

_____

_____

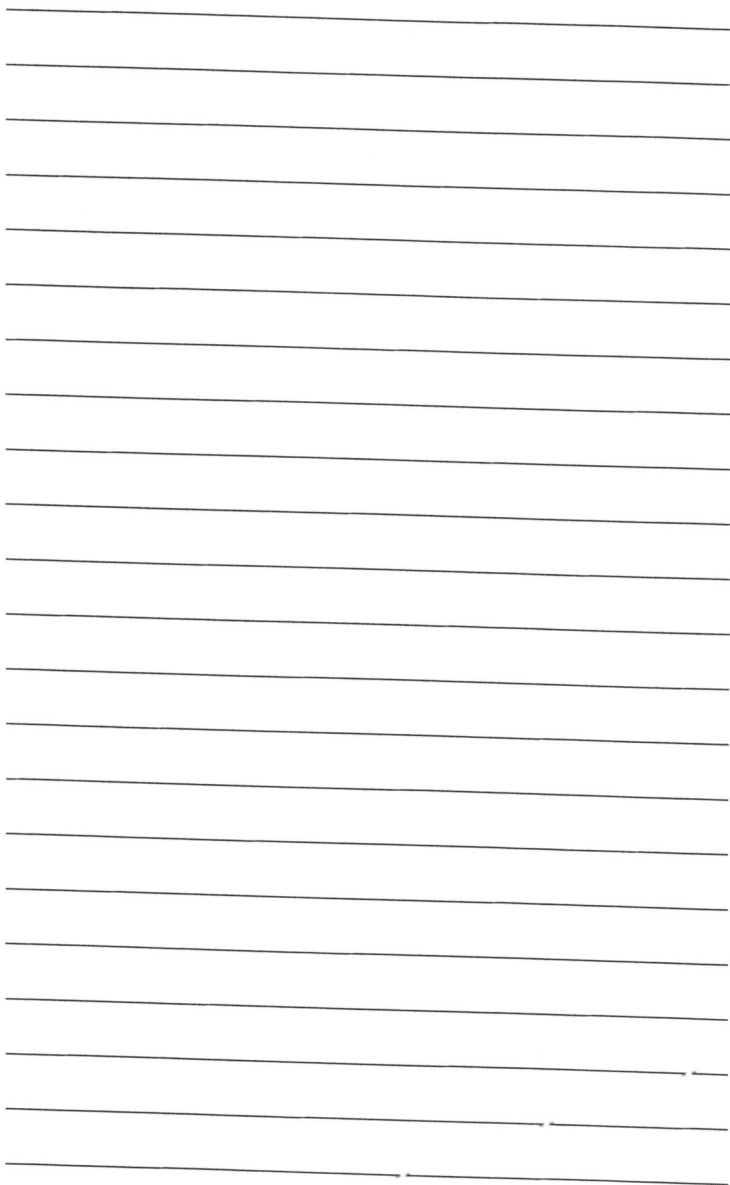

QUOTES

(From Min. Shauna-kaye Brown)

1. With a strong enough desire, you can push past your fears.

2. Fear is our projected imagination that operates to frighten us.

3. It is wise to surround yourself with people who have already done the things you wish to accomplish. In that way, you avoid the pitfalls and you learn the art of achievement.

4. When you are at death's door and you reflect upon your life, your reflection should be that of a life well lived without regrets.

5. Adversity connotes unfavourable circumstances such has, hard times, failure, and misfortune. However, these do not define you. What defines you is your ability to overcome.

6. Make a deliberate effort today and every day henceforth to work on God's purpose for your life.

7. One of the most difficult things to do is overcome a tragedy but if you can do that you can do almost anything.

8. It is a travesty to mentally succumb to life's tragedies because in doing so you hasten the death of your greatness even as you continue to just exist.

9. Do not be afraid to pave new paths, remember the one you now follow was paved by those who went before you.

10. Embrace your difference, it is a statement of who you are. The status quo exists because someone else chose to be different.

11. We do not know for how long we will live but for as long as we do, we should endeavour to maximize our potential!

12. To be realistic about the pursuit of your dreams is to be resilient, dedicated and famished for the success you seek. You must be prepared to become uncomfortable in your current situation such that you want nothing more than to be far removed from it.

13. Winning requires endurance if you abandon the race before the finish line you will never know how it would have ended."

14. To achieve success, you must be deliberate about the pursuit of your dreams. Success is scarcely a chance occurrence.

15. Fitness is a part of becoming the best you.

16. It is necessary for you to improve all areas of your life as you seek to become a better you.

17. To be successful you have to stay in the game.

18. Mental strength is necessary for one to progress. Without this characteristic, we inevitably make ourselves less effective.

19. "What you do NOW will determine the life you live tomorrow.

20. "You have it in you to create the life you want; only then will you have the life you deserve.

ABOUT THE AUTHOR

Shauna-kaye Brown is a Minister, Speaker, and Author who specializes in Personal Transformation. She is an Attorney-at-Law and Human Services Professional who also holds a dual degree in International Relations and Political Science.

She sees personal transformation as an individual mandate and endeavors to help people make that transition from merely existing to becoming God-realized. She has also made it her personal responsibility to become fortified in the word of God. Hence, she is currently enrolled in Bible School pursuing a Ph.D. in Theology.

Shauna-kaye is of the fervent belief that God is calling disciples to remind the nations of His imminent coming. To successfully lead others to God, she has chosen to be a change-maker. This conviction led her to become a Personal Transformation Strategist as she recognizes the fact that transformation starts from within. People sometimes need to be motivated, encouraged, empowered or equipped and she believes she can help them achieve these outcomes.

Her passion for helping people has led her to many platforms of empowerment through speaking, working with the homeless and teaching the word of God. For Shauna-kaye, the journey is characterized by leading a purpose-driven life, and she is on a quest to win souls in the process.

HIRE SHAUNA-KAYE:

To hire Shauna-kaye for speaking engagements and coaching, email her at shaunakbrownspeaks@gmail.com or visit her website, http://www.shaunakbrownspeaks.com

ALSO BY AUTHOR

The Strategic Goal Setting Handbook

http://bit.ly/StrategicGoalSettingBook

Courageous World Catalysts

http://bit.ly/CourageousWorldCatalystsBook

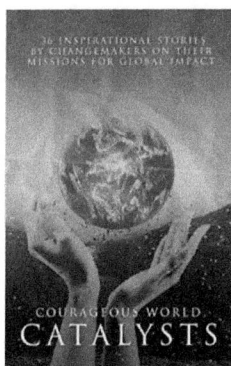